Southern Living.

The SOUTHERN HERITAGE COOKBOOK LIBRARY

Pure Candies Our Specialt

The SOUTHERN HERITAGE
Gift
Receipts
COOKBOOK

OXMOOR HOUSE
Birmingham, Alabama

Southern Living

The Southern Heritage Cookbook Library

Copyright 1985 by Oxmoor House, Inc.
Book Division of Southern Progress Corporation
P.O. Box 2463, Birmingham, Alabama 35201

Southern Living® is a federally registered trademark belonging to
Southern Living, Inc.

Library of Congress Catalog Number: 85-080346
ISBN: 0-8487-0615-3

Manufactured in the United States of America

The Southern Heritage GIFT RECEIPTS Cookbook

Executive Editor: Ann H. Harvey
Southern Living® Foods Editor: Jean W. Liles
Senior Editor: Joan E. Denman
Senior Foods Editor: Katherine M. Eakin
Assistant Editor: Ellen de Lathouder
Assistant Foods Editor: Helen R. Turk
Director, Test Kitchen: Laura N. Massey
Test Kitchen Home Economists: Kay E. Clarke, Rebecca J. Riddle,
   Elizabeth J. Taliaferro, Dee Waller, Elise Wright Walker
Production Manager: Jerry R. Higdon
Copy Editor: Melinda E. West
Editorial Assistants: Mary Ann Laurens, Karen P. Traccarella,
   Donna A. Rumbarger
Food Photographer: Jim Bathie
Food Stylist: Sara Jane Ball
Layout Designer: Christian von Rosenvinge
Mechanical Artist: Faith Nance
Research Editors: Alicia Hathaway, Philip Napoli

Special Consultants

Art Director: Irwin Glusker
Heritage Consultant: Meryle Evans
Foods Writer: Lillian B. Marshall
Food and Recipe Consultants: Marilyn Wyrick Ingram,
   Audrey P. Stehle

Cover (front row from left): Wine Jelly (page 16), Strawberry Preserves
(page 19), Orange Marmalade (page 21), Bourbon Bonbons (page 134),
Double Peanut Clusters (page 136), Lollipops (page 111), and assorted
pickles. Back row from left: Peanut Brittle Wreath (page 112), Dried
Fruit in Rum (page 84), Divinity Fudge (page 100), and assorted vinegars.

Collection of Bonnie Slotnick

CONTENTS

Sweeten the holidays (front row from left): Pecan Crunch (page 112), Chocolate Pecan Logs (page 134). Center: Vanilla Sugar (page 62) and Cinnamon Sugar (page 62). Back row from left: Cinnamon Walnuts (page 96), Zucchini Pickles (page 45), Apple Jelly (page 10), and Creole Pralines (page 127).

INTRODUCTION

The enthusiasm with which we look forward to the holidays has much to do with our state of preparedness. It is with a sinking heart and not a little envy that we respond to those friends who confide in September that they have everything ready and wrapped for Christmas and are, even as they speak, composing their first December party menu. Such serenity of spirit! How do they do it? Well, there are people, not necessarily the same ones, who do beautiful needlework and those who do beautiful food. And they do it year 'round. This book is about the food we can accumulate, not just for holiday gifts, but for any-time-of-year gifts as well. To present gifts from our kitchens in times of joy and sorrow has always been the Southern way of saying "thank you," "I care," or "you're special."

The chapters move from summer fruits for preserving through fall harvests of vegetables and fruits for making pickles and relishes. There are make-anytime condiments that keep well and will be a welcome boost to your friends' gourmet-kitchen arsenals. Candies, for those who are chronically fond of making them, complete the chapters.

These foods, sweet, sour, jellied, brandied, and candied, are available to every one of us; admittedly more so to those who live closest to the gardens and orchards of the South. For friends outside the region, specialties such as the many variations on pecans will be more precious than pearls, as they can only come from the South. Homemade candy and dried figs are more commonly made in our region than in others, so they're prime for shipping elsewhere.

It's the glass-jarred goodies, such as the sugar- and vinegar-preserved goodies, with which we honor our nearby friends, hand carrying them in gay guises of ribbons, bows, and baskets, sometimes with crocheted doily frills tied over the tops. (The latter presentation takes a doubly skilled donor who puts the rest of us to shame by preserving in the morning and needleworking in the afternoon.) Whatever our level of skill, there are recipes in this book for us all. Gifts from our kitchen will be prized, not just because they are truly delicious, but because we made them, and they are part and parcel of that larger more precious gift: our brand of Southern hospitality.

PRESERVED FAVORS

For most of us, sugar has always been plentiful enough to provide us with the sweet jellied fruits we spread so liberally over our hot biscuits and toast. A bumper harvest of berries and fruits needs only another hundred pounds of sugar from the grocer to assure that a family and everyone on its gift list will have a supply of jellies, jams, preserves, butters, and conserves to brighten up their winter.

This accessibility to a sweetener was not always so. Early Southern farmers planted extensive orchards; peach and apple trees by the thousands bore fruit used for drying and as much preserving as the sugar supply would support. But many planters ended up shaking bushels of fruit from their trees to feed to livestock because double-refined sugar was terribly expensive. Even harder to come by was pure sugar-house syrup, which, according to Mary Randolph in *The Virginia Housewife*, 1824, "never ferments and the trouble is very much lessened by having ready-made syrup."

Hannah Glasse, in *The Art of Cookery*, 1796, makes clear that pectin is necessary to cause jelling. Her oranges to be preserved are put in glass or white stone jars after cooking, and a jelly "very strong of the pippin" is poured over them. For years thereafter, cookbooks would give directions for making pectin from apples or the white part of the orange rind. Only in this century came commercial packages and bottles of fruit pectin, which congeal almost any liquid, enabling us even to jell assorted colored wines as gifts.

In the early 1900s, a home canning bulletin with recipes for homemade pectin introduced covering the jar with hot paraffin as a method of sealing jellies and other preserves. Paraffin is now being abandoned by some authorities in favor of the boiling-water bath.

There is a definite link between preserving and the holidays to come. A few measures of "Deck the Halls" might be in order and thoughts of bright paper and ribbons, even in hot weather, during all those sweet makings. Before you begin, don't forget that you'll need pectin (commercial for some recipes), and back up the "sheeting" test with a candy thermometer to determine the jelling point, which usually occurs eight degrees above the boiling point.

There's more than a hint of the season to come in this summer garden setting. Clockwise from rear: Christmas Jam, Favorite Tomato Preserves, Raspberry Jam, and Basil Jelly.

SPECIAL JELLIES

APPLE JELLY

1 quart apple juice
2 tablespoons freshly squeezed lemon juice
1 (1¾-ounce) package powdered fruit pectin
3 cups sugar

Combine apple juice, lemon juice, and powdered pectin in a flat-bottomed kettle, stirring well; bring to a rolling boil, stirring constantly. Add sugar, and return to a rolling boil. Boil 1 minute, stirring constantly. Remove from heat, and skim off foam with a metal spoon.

Quickly ladle hot jelly into hot sterilized jars, leaving ¼-inch headspace. Cover at once with metal lids, and screw bands tight. Process jelly in boiling-water bath 5 minutes. Yield: 4 half pints.

APPLE-RASPBERRY JELLY

2½ cups apple juice
1 cup raspberry juice
1 (1¾-ounce) package powdered fruit pectin
4½ cups sugar

Combine apple juice, raspberry juice, and powdered pectin in a flat-bottomed kettle, stirring well; bring to a rolling boil, stirring constantly. Add sugar, and return to a rolling boil. Boil 1 minute, stirring constantly. Remove from heat, and skim off foam with a metal spoon.

Quickly ladle jelly into hot sterilized jars, leaving ¼-inch headspace. Cover with metal lids, and screw bands tight. Process in boiling-water bath 5 minutes. Yield: 4 half pints.

BLACKBERRY JELLY

3½ cups blackberry juice
1 (1¾-ounce) package powdered fruit pectin
4½ cups sugar

Combine blackberry juice and powdered pectin in a flat-bottomed kettle, stirring well; bring to a rolling boil, stirring constantly. Add sugar; return to a rolling boil. Boil 1 minute, stirring constantly. Remove from heat; skim off foam.

Quickly ladle jelly into hot sterilized jars, leaving ¼-inch headspace. Cover with metal lids, and screw bands tight. Process jelly in boiling-water bath 5 minutes. Yield: 5 half pints.

Note: If jelly is too soft, use ¼ to ½ cup less juice in the next batch. If jelly is too firm, use ¼ to ½ cup more juice.

CRAB APPLE JELLY

3 pounds crab apples, stemmed and coarsely chopped
3 cups water
4 cups sugar

Combine crab apples and water in a flat-bottomed kettle; bring to a boil. Reduce heat; cover and simmer 25 minutes or until fruit is soft. Strain fruit through a jelly bag or 4 layers of cheesecloth, reserving 1 quart juice. Discard pulp.

Return reserved juice and sugar to kettle; stir well. Bring to a rolling boil, stirring frequently. Boil until mixture registers 220° on a candy thermometer or until mixture sheets from a cold metal spoon. Remove from heat, and skim off foam with a metal spoon.

Quickly ladle jelly into hot sterilized jars, leaving ¼-inch headspace. Cover at once with metal lids, and screw bands tight. Process jelly in boiling-water bath 5 minutes. Yield: 6 half pints.

Collection of Bonnie Slotnick

Crab Apple Jelly.

MUSCADINE GRAPE JELLY

1 quart muscadine grape juice
¼ cup lemon juice
7 cups sugar
2 (3-ounce) packages liquid fruit pectin

Combine grape juice, lemon juice, and sugar in a flat-bottomed kettle. Bring to a rolling boil. Add liquid pectin, and return to a boil. Boil 1 minute, stirring constantly. Remove from heat, and skim off foam with a metal spoon.

Ladle hot jelly into hot sterilized jars, leaving ¼-inch headspace. Cover with metal lids, and screw bands tight. Process jelly in boiling-water bath 5 minutes. Yield: 7 half pints.

World War I poster promoted the conservation of food, c.1916. Many World War II posters promoted victory gardens.

GRAPE JELLY

3 cups grape juice
¼ cup lemon juice
1 (1¾-ounce) package
　powdered fruit pectin
4½ cups sugar

Combine grape juice, lemon juice, and powdered fruit pectin in a flat-bottomed kettle, stirring well; bring to a rolling boil, stirring constantly. Add sugar, and return mixture to a rolling boil. Boil 1 minute, stirring constantly. Remove from heat, and skim off foam with a metal spoon.

Quickly ladle hot jelly into hot sterilized jars, leaving ¼-inch headspace. Cover at once with metal lids, and screw bands tight. Process jelly in boiling-water bath 5 minutes. Yield: 5 half pints.

KUMQUAT JELLY

1 quart kumquats (about 4
　dozen)
3½ cups water
⅛ teaspoon baking
　soda
2 cups sugar

Lightly scrape outer skin of kumquats with blade of a knife to release citrus oils. Cut kumquats into thin slices.

Combine kumquats, water, and soda in a flat-bottomed kettle; bring to a boil. Reduce heat; cover and simmer 15 minutes. Set aside to soak overnight. (Do not drain.)

Strain kumquats through a damp jelly bag or 4 layers of cheesecloth, reserving 3 cups juice. Discard pulp.

Combine reserved juice and sugar in kettle; bring to a rolling boil, stirring constantly. Boil, stirring frequently, until mixture registers 220° on a candy thermometer or until mixture sheets from a cold metal spoon. Remove from heat, and skim off foam with a metal spoon.

Quickly ladle jelly into hot sterilized jars, leaving ¼-inch headspace. Cover with metal lids, and screw bands tight. Process jelly in boiling-water bath 5 minutes. Yield: 2 half pints.

*Grape Jelly, gaily
beribboned and slipped
into a cleverly tied paper
bag, is a winning gift.*

RED PLUM JELLY

5½ cups red plum juice
1 (1¾-ounce) package
**   powdered fruit pectin**
7½ cups sugar

Combine plum juice and powdered pectin in a flat-bottomed kettle, stirring well; bring to a rolling boil, stirring constantly. Add sugar, and return to a rolling boil. Boil 1 minute, stirring constantly. Remove from heat, and skim off foam with a metal spoon.

Quickly ladle jelly into hot sterilized jars, leaving ¼-inch headspace. Cover with metal lids, and screw bands tight. Process jelly in boiling-water bath 5 minutes. Yield: 5 half pints.

STRAWBERRY JELLY

3 quarts fresh strawberries,
**   washed and hulled**
½ cup water
¼ cup lemon juice
7½ cups sugar
2 (3-ounce) packages liquid
**   fruit pectin**

Combine strawberries and water in a flat-bottomed kettle; crush berries. Cover and bring to a boil. Reduce heat, and simmer, uncovered, 10 minutes, stirring frequently. Strain berries through a damp jelly bag, reserving 3¾ cups juice. Discard pulp.

Combine reserved juice, lemon juice, and sugar in kettle. Bring to a rolling boil, stirring constantly. Add liquid pectin, and return to a boil. Boil 1 minute, stirring constantly. Remove from heat; skim off foam with a metal spoon.

Quickly ladle jelly into hot sterilized jars, leaving ¼-inch headspace. Cover with metal lids, and screw bands tight. Process in boiling-water bath 5 minutes. Yield: 8 half pints.

Both: Collection of Bonnie Slotnick

If you ever, as a child, ate your fill of unripe apples and later came down with colic, you'd had an overdose of pectin, that magic ingredient most prevalent in apples and citrus peel that makes jelly jell. And if you had a very old Irish grandmother to diagnose the illness, she'd have told you about the legendary pooka, the fairy that makes fruit juices jell. Next to the way it holds its shape, we look for clarity and perfect flavor in jelly. There is more pectin in underripe than in overripe fruit; a balance between pectin and acid is necessary. Commercial pectin takes the guesswork out of jelly making. When you present your favorite jellies, tie a spoon into the ribbon.

Certo Ad shows flavorful fruits, 1927.

JALAPEÑO PEPPER JELLY

GREEN PEPPER JELLY

6 large green peppers, seeded, coarsely chopped, and divided
1½ cups vinegar, divided
6 cups sugar
1½ teaspoons crushed red pepper
½ teaspoon salt
2 (3-ounce) packages liquid fruit pectin
Green liquid food coloring

Place half of chopped pepper and ¾ cup vinegar in container of an electric blender; process until blended. Repeat procedure with remaining chopped peppers and vinegar.

Place pepper mixture in a flat-bottomed kettle; bring to a boil. Reduce heat; cover and simmer until peppers are tender. Drain. Reserve juice; discard pulp.

Combine reserved juice, sugar, red pepper, and salt in kettle. Bring to a rolling boil. Add liquid pectin, and return to a boil. Boil 1 minute, stirring constantly. Remove from heat, and skim off foam with a metal spoon. Stir in food coloring, 1 drop at a time, to reach desired color.

Quickly ladle jelly into hot sterilized jars, leaving ¼-inch headspace. Cover with metal lids, and screw bands tight. Process jelly in boiling-water bath 5 minutes. Yield: 5 half pints.

Green Pepper Jelly (left) or Jalapeño Pepper Jelly can turn cream cheese into an hors d'oeuvre.

2 large green peppers, seeded and finely chopped
8 fresh jalapeño peppers, finely chopped
6⅓ cups sugar
1⅓ cups white vinegar
3 tablespoons fresh lime juice
2 (3-ounce) packages liquid fruit pectin
Green or red liquid food coloring

Combine peppers, sugar, vinegar, and lime juice in a flat-bottomed kettle; stir well. Bring to a rolling boil, and boil 1 minute, stirring constantly. Add liquid fruit pectin, and return to a rolling boil. Boil 1 minute, stirring constantly to prevent sticking. Remove from heat, and skim off foam with a metal spoon. Add food coloring, 1 drop at a time, for desired color.

Quickly ladle jelly into hot sterilized jars, leaving ¼-inch headspace. Cover at once with metal lids, and screw bands tight. Process jelly in boiling-water bath 5 minutes. Yield: 6 half pints.

Note: Turn jars frequently during cooling to distribute peppers evenly throughout jelly.

A tower of preserved goods at a Florida show, 1933.

BASIL JELLY

½ cup fresh basil leaves,
  crushed
3¼ cups sugar
½ cup vinegar
1 cup water
2 drops green food coloring
1 (3-ounce) package liquid
  fruit pectin

Tie basil in cheesecloth; set aside. Combine sugar, vinegar, water, and food coloring in a flat-bottomed kettle, stirring well; add reserved basil. Bring to a rolling boil, stirring constantly; add liquid pectin, and return to a rolling boil. Boil 1 minute, stirring constantly. Remove from heat, and discard basil. Skim off foam with a metal spoon.

Quickly ladle jelly into hot sterilized jars, leaving ¼-inch headspace. Cover at once with metal lids, and screw bands tight. Process jelly in boiling-water bath 5 minutes. Serve with roast beef or pork. Yield: 3 half pints.

MINT JELLY

1 cup chopped fresh mint
  leaves
1 cup water
½ cup vinegar
3½ cups sugar
Green food coloring
1 (3-ounce) package liquid
  fruit pectin

Combine mint, water, vinegar, and sugar in a flat-bottomed kettle, stirring well; bring to a rolling boil, stirring constantly. Remove from heat, and strain through a sieve. Discard mint leaves.

Return strained liquid to kettle. Stir in food coloring, 1 drop at a time, until desired color is reached. Bring to a rolling boil. Add liquid pectin, and return to a rolling boil. Boil 1 minute, stirring constantly. Remove from heat, and skim off foam with a metal spoon.

Quickly ladle jelly into hot sterilized jars, leaving ¼-inch headspace. Cover with metal lids, and screw bands tight.

Process jelly in boiling-water bath 5 minutes. Serve with lamb or other meats. Yield: 1½ pints or 3 half pints.

Note: Let Mint Jelly stand at least one week to allow flavor to intensify.

PINK CHAMPAGNE JELLY

3 cups pink champagne
¾ cup water
1 (1¾-ounce) package
  powdered fruit pectin
4 cups sugar

Combine champagne, water, and powdered pectin in a flat-bottomed kettle; bring to a rolling boil, stirring constantly. Add sugar; return to a rolling boil. Boil 1 minute, stirring constantly. Remove from heat; skim off foam.

Quickly ladle jelly into hot sterilized jars, leaving ¼-inch headspace. Cover with metal lids, and screw bands tight. Process in boiling-water bath 5 minutes. Yield: 5 half pints.

WINE JELLY

2 cups Burgundy, port, or
  sherry wine
2 cups sugar
1 (3-ounce) package liquid
  fruit pectin

Combine wine and sugar in a flat-bottomed kettle. Bring to a rolling boil, stirring frequently. Add liquid pectin, and return to a rolling boil. Boil 1 minute, stirring constantly. Remove from heat; skim off foam with a metal spoon.

Quickly ladle jelly into hot sterilized jars, leaving ¼-inch headspace. Cover at once with metal lids, and screw bands tight. Process jelly in boiling-water bath 5 minutes. Yield: about 3 half pints.

Note: Wine Jelly may be poured into hot sterilized wine glasses; seal with a ⅛-inch layer of paraffin. Store in refrigerator until ready to use.

A rich harvest of grapes in Virginia, c.1925.

Virginia State Library

PRESERVES AND MARMALADES

The latest technique in cherry-pitting on a trade card, c.1890; truly a useful invention.

CHERRY PRESERVES

2 pounds pitted, tart red
  cherries
4 cups sugar

Combine cherries and sugar in a flat-bottomed kettle; mix well, and let stand 3 to 4 hours.

Slowly bring cherry mixture to a boil, stirring until sugar dissolves. Boil, stirring frequently, 15 minutes or until cherries become glossy. Remove from heat, and skim off foam with a metal spoon.

Remove cherries from syrup with a slotted spoon, and place in a shallow pan. Bring syrup to a boil; cook, stirring frequently, 10 minutes or until syrup has thickened to desired consistency. Pour syrup over cherries. Let stand, uncovered, 12 to 24 hours in a cool place. Shake pan occasionally so that the cherries will absorb the syrup and remain plump and whole. (Do not stir.)

Ladle preserves into hot sterilized jars, leaving ¼-inch headspace. Cover at once with metal lids, and screw bands tight. Process preserves in boiling-water bath 15 minutes. Yield: 4 half pints.

FIG PRESERVES

12 pounds fresh figs
1 cup baking soda
8 cups sugar
2 quarts water

Place figs in a large shallow container; sprinkle with soda. Cover with boiling water, and let stand 5 minutes. Rinse and drain in 2 baths of clean, cold water. Set aside.

Combine sugar and 2 quarts water in a flat-bottomed kettle; bring to a boil over medium heat, stirring constantly until sugar dissolves. Add reserved figs; return to a boil. Boil, stirring frequently, 25 minutes or until figs become tender and translucent.

Remove figs from syrup with a slotted spoon; boil syrup an additional 10 minutes or until desired consistency. Return figs to syrup. Remove from heat, and skim off foam with a metal spoon.

Quickly ladle preserves into hot sterilized jars, leaving ¼-inch headspace. Cover at once with metal lids, and screw bands tight. Process preserves in boiling-water bath 15 minutes. Yield: about 15 half pints.

PEACH PRESERVES

1 pound sliced, peeled
  peaches
1½ cups sugar
½ cup water
1 tablespoon lemon juice

Combine peaches, sugar, water, and lemon juice in a flat-bottomed kettle; slowly bring to a boil. Boil, stirring frequently, until peaches become translucent and mixture registers 220° on a candy thermometer or until mixture sheets from a cold metal spoon. Remove from heat, and skim off foam with a metal spoon.

Quickly ladle preserves into hot sterilized jars, leaving a ¼-inch headspace. Cover at once with metal lids, and screw bands tight. Process preserves in boiling-water bath 15 minutes. Yield: 2 half pints.

PEAR PRESERVES

1 pound pears, peeled, cored, and chopped
1½ cups sugar
¾ cup water

Place pears in a small saucepan; add water to cover. Bring to a boil. Reduce heat; cover and cook 15 minutes or until pears are tender. Drain well, and set aside.

Combine sugar and water in Dutch oven; cook over low heat, stirring occasionally, until sugar dissolves. Add reserved pears, and bring to a rolling boil. Boil, stirring frequently, until pears become translucent. Remove from heat, and skim off foam with a metal spoon.

Quickly ladle preserves into hot sterilized jars, leaving ¼-inch headspace. Cover at once with metal lids, and screw bands tight. Process in boiling-water bath 15 minutes. Yield: about 7 half pints.

RASPBERRY PRESERVES

2 cups fresh raspberries, washed and drained
2 cups sugar

Combine raspberries and sugar in a medium saucepan; slowly bring to a boil, stirring frequently. Boil, stirring occasionally, 8 to 10 minutes or until mixture thickens. Remove from heat, and skim off foam with a metal spoon.

Quickly ladle preserves into hot sterilized jars, leaving ¼-inch headspace. Cover at once with metal lids, and screw bands tight. Process preserves in boiling-water bath 15 minutes. Yield: 2 half pints.

Pear preserves are nowhere more popular than in the South, and for good reason: most authorities agree that pears grown in the Southeast hold their shape better in canning and preserving than pears grown elsewhere. Pears are too low in pectin to make good jelly, but pear preserves have been a staple on our tables for generations. The old-time preserving method consisted of alternating layers of sliced pears and sugar (one pound fruit to three-fourths pound sugar) in the preserving kettle and letting it stand overnight. In the morning, the pears were cooked in their juice and sealed in jars.

An engraving of raspberry picking, Harpers Weekly, 1873.

Strawberry-Lemon Preserves are nestled in a wreath of tissue paper and strawberries.

STRAWBERRY PRESERVES

1½ quarts fresh strawberries, washed and hulled
5 cups sugar
⅓ cup lemon juice

Combine strawberries and sugar in a flat-bottomed kettle; mix well, and let stand 3 to 4 hours.

Slowly bring strawberry mixture to a boil, stirring until sugar dissolves. Add lemon juice. Boil, stirring occasionally, 12 minutes or until berries become translucent. Remove from heat; skim off foam with a metal spoon.

Remove strawberries from syrup with a slotted spoon, and place in a shallow pan. Bring syrup to a boil; boil, stirring frequently, 10 minutes or until desired consistency. Pour syrup over strawberries. Let stand, uncovered, 12 to 24 hours in a cool place. Shake pan occasionally so berries will absorb the syrup and remain plump and whole. (Do not stir.) Skim off foam with a metal spoon.

Ladle preserves into hot sterilized jars, leaving ¼-inch headspace. Cover at once with metal lids, and screw bands tight. Process preserves in boiling-water bath 15 minutes. Yield: 4 half pints.

Collection of Bonnie Slotnick

STRAWBERRY-LEMON PRESERVES

1 lemon
2 quarts strawberries, washed and hulled
¼ cup water
1 (1¾-ounce) package powdered fruit pectin
6½ cups sugar

Scrape outer surface of lemon with blade of a knife to release citrus oils. Cut lemon into quarters, discarding seeds. Place lemon in container of an electric blender, and process until well ground.

Combine ground lemon, strawberries, water, and powdered pectin in a flat-bottomed kettle. Bring to a rolling boil, stirring gently. Add sugar, and return to a rolling boil. Boil 1 minute, stirring constantly. Remove from heat, and skim off foam with a metal spoon. Stir gently 3 to 5 minutes to distribute fruit evenly.

Quickly ladle preserves into hot sterilized jars, leaving ¼-inch headspace. Cover at once with metal lids, and screw bands tight. Process preserves in boiling-water bath 15 minutes. Yield: 11 half pints.

WATERMELON RIND PRESERVES

1½ quarts watermelon rind, peeled and cut into 1-inch cubes
¼ cup salt
2 quarts cold water
2 teaspoons ground ginger
4 cups sugar
¼ cup lemon juice
7 cups water
1 lemon, thinly sliced and seeded

Combine rind, salt, and cold water in a large glass container. Cover and let stand at room temperature 5 to 6 hours. Rinse and drain in 2 baths of cold water. Cover with cold water; let stand 30 minutes. Drain.

Place rind in a flat-bottomed kettle; sprinkle with ginger, and add water to cover. Bring to a boil. Reduce heat; simmer, stirring occasionally, 15 minutes or until tender. Drain.

Combine sugar, lemon juice, and 7 cups water in a stainless steel saucepan. Bring to a boil; boil 5 minutes, stirring frequently. Add rind, and boil gently 30 minutes, stirring occasionally. Add lemon slices; reduce heat, and simmer, stirring occasionally, 25 minutes or until lemon slices are tender.

Ladle preserves into hot sterilized jars, leaving ¼-inch headspace. Cover with metal lids; screw bands tight. Process in boiling-water bath 15 minutes. Yield: 6 half pints.

FAVORITE TOMATO PRESERVES

5 pounds small, firm tomatoes, peeled and cored
8 cups sugar
3 lemons
3 (⅛-inch-thick) slices gingerroot
1 (3-inch) stick cinnamon
¼ teaspoon salt

Place whole tomatoes in a large glass mixing bowl, and sprinkle with sugar. Cover and refrigerate overnight.

Drain mixture, reserving tomatoes and liquid. Place liquid and any undissolved sugar in a flat-bottomed kettle; stir well. Bring to a rolling boil; boil, stirring occasionally, until mixture registers 230° on a candy thermometer or until mixture thickens.

Scrape outer surface of lemons with blade of a knife to release citrus oils. Cut lemons into thin slices, discarding seeds. Add lemon slices, tomatoes, gingerroot, cinnamon, and salt to syrup mixture, mixing well. Bring to a boil; boil, stirring frequently, until tomatoes become translucent. Discard gingerroot and cinnamon.

Quickly ladle preserves into hot sterilized jars, leaving ¼-inch headspace. Cover at once with metal lids, and screw bands tight. Process preserves in boiling-water bath 15 minutes. Yield: 5 pints.

From Burpee & Co., 1914, a new two-serving size watermelon.

BURPEE'S
NEW
WATERMELON
BABY-
DELIGHT"

"A
WHOLE C
FOR TW

W. ATLEE BURPEE & CO., PHILADELPHIA

COPYRIGHT 1914 B
W. ATLEE BURPEE & C
PHILADELPHIA

Orange Marmalade (left) and Rhubarb Marmalade: the sweetness saved up for another season.

APRICOT-ORANGE MARMALADE

2 (16-ounce) packages dried
  apricots
12 medium oranges
1 large grapefruit
1 gallon water, divided
½ teaspoon baking soda
1¾ cups crushed pineapple,
  drained
¾ cup lemon juice
9 cups sugar

Place apricots in a large mixing bowl with water to cover; soak overnight.

Lightly scrape outer skins of oranges and grapefruit with blade of a knife to release citrus oils. Peel oranges and grapefruit; chop rind (reserve pulp for other uses).

Combine chopped rind, 2 quarts water, and soda in a large stainless steel saucepan; bring to a boil. Reduce heat; cover and simmer 15 minutes. Rinse well; drain.

Add remaining water to rind mixture in saucepan; bring to a boil. Reduce heat; cover and simmer 15 minutes. Remove from heat. Keep covered, and let rind stand in cooking liquid overnight. Drain well.

Drain and mince apricots. Place in a flat-bottomed kettle. Add crushed pineapple, lemon juice, sugar, and orange and grapefruit rind, stirring well. Slowly bring to a boil, stirring until sugar dissolves. Boil, stirring constantly, until mixture registers 220° on a candy thermometer or until mixture sheets from a cold metal spoon. Remove from heat, and skim off foam with a metal spoon.

Quickly ladle marmalade into hot sterilized jars, leaving ¼-inch headspace. Cover at once with metal lids, and screw bands tight. Process marmalade in boiling-water bath 10 minutes. Yield: 18 half pints.

ORANGE MARMALADE

4 medium oranges
1½ quarts water,
  divided
¼ teaspoon baking soda
3 cups sugar

Scrape outer skins of oranges with blade of a knife to release citrus oils. Peel oranges, and grind rind; reserve pulp. Combine ground orange rind, 3 cups water, and soda in a medium-size stainless steel saucepan; bring to a boil. Reduce heat; cover and simmer 5 minutes. Rinse well; drain.

Combine remaining 3 cups water and orange rind in saucepan; bring to a boil. Reduce heat; cover and simmer 15 minutes. Let stand in cooking liquid overnight. (Do not drain.)

Cut reserved orange pulp into quarters; remove and discard seeds. Place pulp in container of an electric blender; process until smooth.

Combine orange rind and liquid, pureed pulp, and sugar in a flat-bottomed kettle; slowly bring to a boil, stirring until sugar dissolves. Boil, stirring constantly, until mixture registers 220° on a candy thermometer or until mixture sheets from a cold metal spoon. Remove from heat, and skim off foam with a metal spoon.

Quickly ladle marmalade into hot sterilized jars, leaving ¼-inch headspace. Cover at once with metal lids, and screw bands tight. Process marmalade in boiling-water bath 10 minutes. Yield: 4 half pints.

ORANGE-LEMON MARMALADE

6 medium oranges
1½ quarts water, divided
¼ teaspoon baking soda
1 cup lemon juice, divided
3 cups sugar

Scrape outer skins of oranges with blade of a knife to release citrus oils. Peel oranges, and grind rind; reserve pulp. Combine ground orange rind, 3 cups water, and soda in a medium-size stainless steel saucepan; bring to a boil. Reduce heat; cover and simmer 15 minutes. Rinse well; drain.

Add remaining water and ½ cup lemon juice to prepared orange rind in saucepan; bring to a boil. Reduce heat; cover and simmer 15 minutes. Let stand in cooking liquid overnight.

Cut reserved orange pulp into quarters; remove and discard seeds. Place pulp in container of an electric blender; process until smooth. Add to orange rind mixture; stir until well blended.

Place 3 cups orange mixture (reserving remainder for other uses) in a flat-bottomed kettle. Add remaining lemon juice and sugar, stirring well. Slowly bring to a boil, stirring until sugar dissolves. Boil, stirring occasionally, until mixture registers 220° on a candy thermometer or until mixture sheets from a cold metal spoon. Remove from heat, and skim off foam with a metal spoon.

Quickly ladle marmalade into hot sterilized jars, leaving ¼-inch headspace. Cover at once with metal lids, and screw bands tight. Process marmalade in boiling-water bath 10 minutes. Yield: 3 half pints.

PEAR MARMALADE MAGNOLIA

1 orange
1 lemon
⅛ teaspoon baking soda
2 pounds pears, peeled and cored
3 cups sugar

Scrape outer surface of orange and lemon with blade of a knife to release citrus oils. Peel orange and lemon, reserving rind. Remove and discard white membrane and seeds from pulp.

Combine orange and lemon rind, soda, and water to cover in a medium-size stainless steel saucepan. Bring to a boil. Reduce heat; simmer 5 minutes, stirring frequently. Drain. Add water to cover; bring to a boil. Boil 5 minutes, stirring frequently. Drain and cool.

Grind together orange and lemon rind, reserved orange and lemon pulp, and pears. Combine fruit and sugar in a flat-bottomed kettle. Bring to a boil. Reduce heat; simmer, stirring frequently, 40 minutes or until mixture thickens. Remove from heat, and skim off foam with a metal spoon.

Quickly ladle marmalade into hot sterilized jars, leaving ¼-inch headspace. Cover at once with metal lids, and screw bands tight. Process marmalade in boiling-water bath 10 minutes. Yield: 5 half pints.

RHUBARB MARMALADE

4 cups rhubarb (about 2 pounds), cut into ½-inch pieces
¾ cup water
1 (1¾-ounce) package powdered fruit pectin
5½ cups sugar

Combine rhubarb, water, and powdered pectin in a flat-bottomed kettle; stir well. Bring to a boil, stirring frequently. Add sugar, and return to a rolling boil. Boil 1 minute, stirring frequently. Remove from heat. Stir 7 minutes; skim off foam with a metal spoon.

Quickly ladle marmalade into hot sterilized jars, leaving ¼-inch headspace. Cover at once with metal lids, and screw bands tight. Process marmalade in boiling-water bath 10 minutes. Yield: 5 half pints.

GREEN TOMATO MARMALADE

4 pounds green tomatoes, peeled and thinly sliced
2 lemons, thinly sliced
6 cups sugar

Place tomatoes in a flat-bottomed kettle. Slowly bring to a boil. Reduce heat; cover and simmer 30 minutes. Add lemon slices and sugar, stirring well. Bring to a boil; boil until mixture registers 220° on a candy thermometer or until mixture sheets from a cold metal spoon. Remove from heat, and skim off foam with a metal spoon.

Quickly ladle marmalade into hot sterilized jars, leaving ¼-inch headspace. Cover at once with metal lids, and screw bands tight. Process marmalade in boiling-water bath 10 minutes. Yield: 6 half pints.

JAMS, BUTTERS, AND HONEY

BLUEBERRY JAM

4½ cups blueberries, crushed
    (about 2 pounds)
3 cups sugar

Combine blueberries and sugar in a flat-bottomed kettle; cook over low heat, stirring until sugar dissolves. Bring to a rolling boil, stirring constantly, until mixture registers 220° on a candy thermometer or until mixture sheets from a cold metal spoon. Remove from heat; skim off foam.

Quickly ladle jam into hot sterilized jars, leaving ¼-inch headspace. Cover at once with metal lids, and screw bands tight. Process jam in boiling-water bath 10 minutes. Yield: 5 half pints.

Note: Blackberries may be substituted for blueberries. If seedless jam is preferred, crushed blackberries may be heated until soft and pressed through a sieve or food mill; add sugar, and proceed as directed.

Blueberry Jam, a lovely surprise for a festive breakfast.

FIG JAM

5 pounds fresh figs
¾ cup water
6 cups sugar
¼ cup lemon juice

Pour boiling water over figs to cover; let stand 10 minutes. Drain well. Remove stems, and chop figs.

Combine figs, water, and sugar in a flat-bottomed kettle; cook over low heat, stirring occasionally, until sugar dissolves. Bring to a rolling boil, stirring constantly, until mixture registers 220° on a candy thermometer or until mixture sheets from a cold metal spoon. Stir in lemon juice, and cook 1 additional minute. Remove from heat, and skim off foam with a metal spoon.

Quickly ladle jam into hot sterilized jars, leaving ¼-inch headspace. Cover at once with metal lids, and screw bands tight. Process jam in boiling-water bath 10 minutes. Yield: 10 pints.

RASPBERRY JAM

2 quarts raspberries, washed
    and drained
⅓ cup water
1 tablespoon grated lemon
    rind
1 tablespoon lemon juice
1 (1¾-ounce) package
    powdered fruit pectin
6 cups sugar

Combine raspberries, water, lemon rind, juice, and powdered pectin in a flat-bottomed kettle; mix well. Bring to a rolling boil, stirring frequently. Add sugar, and return to a rolling boil. Boil 1 minute, stirring constantly. Remove from heat, and skim off foam with a metal spoon.

Ladle jam into hot sterilized jars, leaving ¼-inch headspace. Cover with metal lids, and screw bands tight. Process jam in boiling-water bath 10 minutes. Yield: 7 half pints.

SPICED PEACH JAM

1 (3-inch) stick cinnamon
1 teaspoon whole cloves
½ teaspoon whole allspice
2 quarts chopped, peeled
  peaches
½ cup water
6 cups sugar

Tie cinnamon, cloves, and allspice in a cheesecloth bag.

Combine peaches and water in a flat-bottomed kettle; cover and simmer 10 minutes. Add sugar and spice bag. Cook over low heat, stirring occasionally, until sugar dissolves. Bring to a rolling boil, stirring constantly, until mixture registers 220° on a candy thermometer or until mixture sheets from a cold metal spoon. Remove from heat, and skim off foam with a metal spoon; discard spice bag.

Quickly ladle jam into hot sterilized jars, leaving ¼-inch headspace. Cover at once with metal lids, and screw bands tight. Process jam in boiling-water bath 10 minutes. Yield: 7 half pints.

STRAWBERRY JAM

3 pounds strawberries,
  washed and hulled
3¾ cups sugar

Combine strawberries and sugar in a flat-bottomed kettle; cook over low heat, stirring until sugar dissolves. Bring to a rolling boil. Boil, stirring and mashing strawberries, until mixture registers 220° on a candy thermometer or until mixture sheets from a cold metal spoon. Cook to a higher temperature for a firmer product, to a lower temperature for a softer product. Remove from heat, and skim off foam.

Quickly ladle jam into hot sterilized jars, leaving ¼-inch headspace. Cover at once with metal lids, and screw bands tight. Process jam in boiling-water bath 10 minutes. Yield: 5 half pints.

STRAWBERRY-ORANGE JAM

4½ cups crushed strawberries
  (about 2 quarts whole
  berries)
2 teaspoons grated orange
  rind
1 (1¾-ounce) package
  powdered fruit pectin
7 cups sugar

Combine crushed strawberries, orange rind, and powdered pectin in a flat-bottomed kettle; mix well. Bring to a rolling boil, stirring constantly. Add sugar, and return to a rolling boil. Boil 1 minute, stirring constantly. Remove from heat, and skim off foam with a metal spoon.

Ladle jam into hot sterilized jars, leaving ¼-inch headspace. Cover with metal lids, and screw bands tight. Process in boiling-water bath 10 minutes. Yield: 8 half pints.

"A Swell Peach."

SIMPSON SPRING CARBONADES,

(PURE FRUIT SODAS.)

BOTTLED FOR FINE FAMILY TRADE.

A peach-flavored drink was promoted on this 1887 trade card featuring "a swell peach."

Companion trade cards, 1882, show the disastrous results of mischief making.

CHRISTMAS JAM

1 (8-ounce) jar maraschino
  cherries, undrained
1 (20-ounce) can pineapple
  chunks, drained
2 (6-ounce) packages dried
  apricots
3½ cups water
6 cups sugar

Drain cherries, reserving juice; cut cherries into quarters, and set aside.

Combine reserved cherry juice, pineapple, apricots, and water in a flat-bottomed kettle; stir well. Let stand 1 hour.

Cook fruit mixture over medium heat 20 minutes or until apricots are tender. Reduce heat; add sugar, stirring occasionally until sugar dissolves. Bring to a boil; boil, stirring frequently, until mixture registers 216° on a candy thermometer. Add reserved cherries, stirring constantly, until mixture registers 220° or until mixture sheets from a cold metal spoon. Remove from heat.

Quickly ladle jam into hot sterilized jars, leaving ¼-inch headspace. Cover at once with metal lids, and screw bands tight. Process in boiling-water bath 5 minutes. Yield: 3½ pints or 7 half pints.

OLD-FASHIONED APPLE BUTTER

6 pounds apples, cored and
  sliced
2 quarts apple cider
3 cups sugar
1½ teaspoons ground
  cinnamon
½ teaspoon ground cloves

Place apple slices and cider in a flat-bottomed kettle. Bring to a boil; cover and cook over medium heat 30 minutes or until apples are tender.

Press apples through a sieve. Return strained pulp to kettle; cook over high heat, stirring constantly, until pulp rounds up in a spoon. Add sugar and spices. Reduce heat to medium. Cook, stirring frequently, 1 hour or until mixture thickens.

Quickly ladle apple butter into hot sterilized jars, leaving ¼-inch headspace. Cover at once with metal lids, and screw bands tight. Process in boiling-water bath 5 minutes. Yield: 10 half pints.

A women's cooking class in North Carolina, c.1921.

GRAPE BUTTER

5 pounds grapes
5 cups sugar
2½ teaspoons ground
  cinnamon
2 teaspoons ground mace
⅛ teaspoon ground cloves

Wash grapes; drain and remove stems. Plunge grapes into rapidly boiling water to cover; boil 2 minutes. Drain well. Slip off grape skins, and grind skins finely, reserving pulp; set aside.

Place pulp in a flat-bottomed kettle; cook over medium heat 10 minutes or until seeds begin to separate from pulp. Press pulp through a sieve to remove seeds; discard seeds.

Return pulp to kettle; add reserved skins and remaining ingredients, stirring well. Cook over medium-low heat, stirring constantly, 30 minutes or until mixture thickens.

Quickly ladle butter into hot sterilized jars, leaving ¼-inch headspace. Cover at once with metal lids, and screw bands tight. Process in boiling-water bath 5 minutes. Yield: about 8 half pints.

Fruit butters have enjoyed a high degree of popularity in the South for two persuasive reasons: they are one of the most delicious spreads we have for our toast and hot biscuits, and they are made from ripe, full-flavored fruits which do not have to be perfect in shape or size to cook up smooth and rich. Grape Butter is convincing enough.

OLD-FASHIONED PEACH BUTTER

2 quarts diced, peeled
  peaches
4 cups sugar

Place half of peaches into container of an electric blender; process until coarsely chopped. Pour into a flat-bottomed kettle. Repeat procedure with remaining peaches. Stir in sugar.

Cook over medium-low heat, stirring frequently, 30 minutes or until mixture thickens.

Quickly ladle butter into hot sterilized jars, leaving ¼-inch headspace. Cover at once with metal lids, and screw bands tight. Process in boiling-water bath 5 minutes. Yield: 8 half pints.

SPICED PLUM BUTTER

2 pounds red plums
½ cup water
4 cups sugar
1 teaspoon ground cinnamon
½ teaspoon ground allspice
¼ teaspoon ground nutmeg
¼ teaspoon ground cloves

Wash plums, and slit each in 3 places, using a paring knife. Combine plums and water in a flat-bottomed kettle. Bring to a boil; boil 30 minutes, stirring frequently. Remove from heat, and press through a sieve. Discard skins and seeds.

Return pulp to kettle, and add remaining ingredients, stirring well. Cook over medium-low heat, stirring constantly, 20 minutes or until mixture thickens.

Quickly ladle butter into hot sterilized jars, leaving ¼-inch headspace. Cover at once with metal lids, and screw bands tight. Process in boiling-water bath 5 minutes. Yield: about 8 half pints.

PEAR HONEY

2 pounds pears, peeled,
  cored, and coarsely ground
½ cup crushed pineapple,
  drained
3 cups sugar
2 teaspoons lemon juice

Combine pears and pineapple in a flat-bottomed kettle. Add sugar and lemon juice, stirring well. Slowly bring to a boil, stirring frequently. Boil over medium-low heat, stirring occasionally, 30 minutes or until pears become translucent.

Ladle honey into hot sterilized jars, leaving ¼-inch headspace. Cover with metal lids, and screw bands tight. Process honey in boiling-water bath 5 minutes. Yield: 3 half pints.

Old-Fashioned Peach Butter (front) and Apple Butter (page 25) are old-time Southern favorites.

CONSERVES

APPLE CONSERVE

2 quarts water
1 tablespoon vinegar
1 tablespoon noniodized
   salt
5 tart cooking apples,
   cored
½ cup water
¼ cup lemon juice
½ cup raisins
1 (1¾-ounce) package
   powdered fruit pectin
5½ cups sugar
½ cup chopped pecans

Combine water, vinegar, and salt in a large glass mixing bowl. Mince apples, and add to water mixture; soak 2 to 5 minutes. Drain apples; rinse well.

Combine apples, ½ cup water, lemon juice, raisins, and powdered fruit pectin in a flat-bottomed kettle; stir well. Quickly bring mixture to a rolling boil, stirring constantly. Add sugar, and return to a rolling boil for 1 additional minute, stirring constantly to prevent scorching. Stir in pecans. Remove from heat, and skim off foam with a cold metal spoon.

Quickly pour conserve into hot sterilized jars, leaving ¼-inch headspace. Cover at once with metal lids, and screw bands tight. Process in boiling-water bath 15 minutes. Yield: 6 half pints.

Unlike jam, made of crushed fruit, or preserves, made of whole or cut-up fruit, a conserve is a jamlike mixture of two or more fruits, sometimes with nuts or raisins (or a combination of both) added for textural contrast. Most fruits can be superstars if preserved in this way; feel free to create almost any combination for delectable gifts.

CRANBERRY CONSERVE

3 quarts cranberries, rinsed
   and drained
4 apples, cored and chopped
2 pounds raisins, ground
2 quarts water
Grated rind and juice of 4
   oranges, divided
12 cups sugar, divided
1½ cups chopped pecans,
   divided

Combine cranberries, apples, raisins, and water in a flat-bottomed kettle. Bring to a boil; reduce heat, and simmer, stirring frequently, 10 minutes or until cranberries are tender. Divide mixture into 4 equal portions.

Return one portion of cranberry mixture to kettle. Add one-fourth of orange rind and juice and 3 cups sugar; stir well. Bring to a boil; boil, stirring frequently, until mixture registers 220° on a candy thermometer or until mixture sheets from a cold metal spoon. Add one-fourth of pecans; stir well. Remove from heat; skim off foam.

Ladle conserve into hot sterilized jars, leaving ¼-inch headspace. Cover with metal lids, and screw bands tight. Process in boiling-water bath 15 minutes. Repeat procedure 3 times, using one-fourth of remaining ingredients each time. Yield: 22 half pints.

An 1890 foldover card for paraffin.

Ad for Duraglass preserving jars features plums, 1948.

PLUM CONSERVE

4 pounds plums, unpeeled, seeded, and chopped
6 cups sugar
1 cup raisins
1½ teaspoons grated lemon rind
¼ cup lemon juice
1 cup walnuts

Combine all ingredients, except walnuts, in a flat-bottomed kettle; stir well. Cover and cook over medium heat 20 minutes or until fruit is tender and mixture thickens. Stir frequently to prevent sticking. Blanch walnuts in boiling water 2 minutes; drain well, and chop. Stir into hot fruit mixture.

Quickly pour conserve into hot sterilized jars, leaving ¼-inch headspace. Cover at once with metal lids, and screw bands tight. Process in boiling-water bath 15 minutes. Yield: about 6 half pints.

RHUBARB-PINEAPPLE CONSERVE

1 orange
3 cups peeled and sliced rhubarb
3 cups crushed pineapple, drained
6 cups sugar

Wash and peel orange, reserving rind and pulp. Discard membrane and seeds. Grind together rind and pulp.

Combine orange rind and pulp with remaining ingredients in a flat-bottomed kettle, stirring well. Bring to a boil. Boil, stirring frequently, until mixture registers 220° on a candy thermometer or until mixture sheets from a cold metal spoon.

Ladle conserve into hot sterilized jars, leaving ¼-inch headspace. Cover with metal lids, and screw bands tight. Process in boiling-water bath 15 minutes. Yield: 6 half pints.

PEACH CONSERVE

1 large orange
¼ cup water
2 quarts peeled and chopped peaches
6½ cups sugar
¾ cup crushed pineapple, drained
½ cup chopped maraschino cherries
3 tablespoons lime juice
½ teaspoon salt
½ teaspoon ground ginger
¼ teaspoon ground mace

Remove rind from orange, leaving half of white pith intact. Cut rind into small pieces; set aside. Section orange; remove and discard seeds. Dice pulp.

Combine orange rind and pulp in a flat-bottomed kettle. Add water; bring to a boil. Reduce heat; cover and simmer, stirring occasionally, 10 minutes or until rind is tender. Stir in remaining ingredients. Cook over medium-high heat, stirring frequently, until mixture registers 220° on a candy thermometer or until mixture sheets from a cold metal spoon. Remove from heat; skim off foam.

Quickly ladle conserve into hot sterilized jars, leaving ¼-inch headspace. Cover at once with metal lids, and screw bands tight. Process in boiling-water bath 15 minutes. Yield: 7 half pints.

PEAR CONSERVE

1 quart coarsely ground, cored, unpeeled pears
3½ cups sugar
1 cup raisins, chopped
Grated rind and juice of 1 lemon
½ cup chopped pecans

Combine all ingredients, except pecans, in a flat-bottomed kettle, stirring well. Cover and cook over medium heat 20 minutes or until fruit is translucent. Stir frequently to prevent sticking. Add pecans. Cook 5 minutes or until mixture thickens, stirring frequently.

Quickly ladle conserve into hot sterilized jars, leaving ¼-inch headspace. Cover at once with metal lids, and screw bands tight. Process in boiling-water bath 15 minutes. Yield: about 6 half pints.

FRESH FRUIT CONSERVE

3 cups finely chopped, peeled
   peaches
3 cups finely chopped
   cantaloupe
4½ cups sugar
1 tablespoon lemon juice
⅓ cup coarsely chopped
   blanched almonds
¼ teaspoon salt
½ teaspoon ground nutmeg
¼ teaspoon grated orange
   rind

Combine peaches and cantaloupe in a flat-bottomed kettle; bring to a boil, stirring constantly. Reduce heat; cover and simmer 10 minutes. Stir in sugar and lemon juice. Return to a boil; boil 12 minutes or until mixture thickens, stirring frequently. Add remaining ingredients. Boil, stirring constantly, until mixture registers 220° on a candy thermometer or until mixture sheets from a cold metal spoon. Remove from heat; skim off foam.

Ladle conserve into hot sterilized jars, leaving ¼-inch headspace. Cover with metal lids, and screw bands tight. Process in boiling-water bath 15 minutes. Yield: 6 half pints.

TEXAS

MARIE

PRIDE OF CUMBERLAND

A view of Allen's plant beds in Oct. The result of abundance of manure and thorough cultivation.

Bunch of Plants Trimmed and Tied Ready for Shipment.

Strawberry varieties from W. F. Allen's 1903 catalog.

STRAWBERRY-PINEAPPLE CONSERVE

1 quart finely chopped fresh
   pineapple
4 cups sugar
1 quart washed and hulled
   strawberries

Combine pineapple and sugar in a large glass mixing bowl, stirring well. Cover and let stand 4 hours.

Place pineapple mixture in a flat-bottomed kettle; cook over low heat, stirring frequently, 30 minutes or until tender. Add strawberries, stirring well. Bring to a rolling boil; boil, stirring frequently, until mixture registers 220° on a candy thermometer or until mixture sheets from a cold metal spoon.

Quickly ladle conserve into hot sterilized jars, leaving ¼-inch headspace. Cover at once with metal lids, and screw bands tight. Process in boiling-water bath 15 minutes. Yield: 6 half pints.

How about wrapping jars filled with the "fruits of our labor" for gift giving? We can always cover the lid of the filled jar with colorful fabric and tie a pert bow around the band. Bags made of wrapping paper are attractive and convenient. Try making your own by duplicating the pattern of a regular brown bag with gift wrap; only glue is needed. Attach a fruit-shaped gift card to the bow. Or present the contents of the jar in a decorative crock or jelly dish with a note that says, "Please refrigerate."

CITRUS CONSERVE

Rind of 1 orange
2 cups water, divided
⅛ teaspoon baking soda
2 cups ground grapefruit pulp
2 cups ground orange pulp
1 cup ground fresh
   cranberries
2 cups sugar
¾ cup chopped pecans
½ cup raisins

Combine orange rind and 1 cup water in container of an electric blender; process until finely chopped. Pour mixture into a small non-aluminum saucepan; add soda, stirring well. Bring to a boil. Reduce heat; cover and simmer 5 minutes. Rinse and drain.

Return orange rind to saucepan; add remaining water. Bring to a boil. Reduce heat; cover and simmer 5 minutes. Set aside to cool.

Combine grapefruit pulp, orange pulp, cranberries, and reserved rind mixture in a flat-bottomed kettle. Bring to a boil; boil 15 minutes, stirring frequently. Stir in sugar, and boil until mixture reaches 220° on a candy thermometer or until mixture sheets from a cold metal spoon. Add pecans and raisins, stirring well. Remove from heat, and skim off foam with a metal spoon.

Quickly ladle conserve into hot sterilized jars, leaving ¼-inch headspace. Cover at once with metal lids, and screw bands tight. Process in boiling-water bath 10 minutes. Yield: 5 half pints.

Citrus Conserve contains a riot of complementary flavors.

HOW TO MAKE JELLY WITHOUT ADDED PECTIN

RASPBERRY JELLY

3 quarts fresh raspberries, washed and
  hulled
½ cup water
½ cup lemon juice
2½ cups sugar

Combine raspberries and water in a flat-bottomed kettle; crush berries. Cover and bring to a boil. Reduce heat; simmer, uncovered, 10 minutes, stirring frequently. Strain berries through a dampened jelly bag, reserving 3½ cups juice; discard pulp.

Combine reserved juice and lemon juice in kettle, stirring well; bring to a rolling boil. Add sugar, stirring until sugar dissolves. Continue to boil until mixture sheets from a cold metal spoon. Remove from heat, and skim off foam with a metal spoon.

Ladle jelly into hot sterilized jars, leaving ¼-inch headspace. Cover at once with metal lids; screw bands tight. Process jelly in boiling-water bath 5 minutes. Yield: 5 half pints.

Step 1 — Place raspberries in a flat-bottomed kettle; add water. Crush berries, using a potato masher. Cover and bring to a boil. Reduce heat; simmer, uncovered, 10 minutes, stirring frequently to prevent scorching.

Step 4 — Boil mixture rapidly until mixture sheets from a cold metal spoon. The sheeting stage (220° to 222° on a candy thermometer) occurs when 2 drops flow together as a single drop from a cold metal spoon.

Step 5 — Remove jelly mixture from heat. Skim off foam from top of jelly, using a cold metal spoon or jelly skimmer. Place a widemouthed funnel over hot sterilized canning jars. Quickly pour hot jelly into jars, leaving ¼-inch headspace.

Step 2 — Line a colander with a dampened jelly bag or 4 layers of cheesecloth. Place colander over a large bowl. Pour cooked raspberries into jelly bag, and suspend the bag. Let juice slowly drip through bag without pressing.

Step 3 — Measure raspberry juice. If measure is less than called for, add water to pulp in bag, and let drain. Pour raspberry juice and lemon juice into a flat-bottomed kettle; bring to a rolling boil. Add sugar, stirring until sugar dissolves.

Step 6 — Wipe jar rims and threads clean with a clean damp cloth. Any jelly remaining on rim can prevent an airtight seal. Cover at once with metal canning lids, and screw bands tight. Invert jars for a few seconds to seal completely.

Step 7 — Place jars on rack in a canner with boiling water to cover 2 inches. Cover canner, and return to a boil; boil gently 5 minutes. Remove jars from canner, and place on a protected surface, away from drafts, to cool.

PICKLES TO PRESENT

The value of pickle — in the broad sense of the term — as a source of minerals and vitamins, especially A and C, is not exactly a recent discovery. To keep his gladiators in top condition, Julius Caesar insisted that pickle be included in their diet, and Cleopatra deemed it the secret of beauty and health. And let's not forget that the threat of scurvy was all but eliminated for the early explorers when they began bringing kegs of pickles on board.

Salt and vinegar at one time in Sparta were the only condiments allowed in food. Thanks to those two basic preservatives, Henry J. Heinz, who started his pickling business in 1869, became famous for his "57 Varieties." Fortunately, he did not know that "all pickles have nearly the same taste, and there is no use (and much trouble) in multiplying varieties . . . ," as claimed by Eliza Leslie in her *New Cookery Book*, 1857. It is doubtful whether Southerners took notice of the Philadelphia writer's comment either; they had too many fruits and vegetables to put up. Besides, she had repudiated beaten biscuit!

But Miss Leslie did know that brass and copper utensils must never be used in pickling; that has not changed. And all the old instructions that require "best" vinegar (5% or 6% acetic acid) and "clear" salt (noniodized) still pertain. But we no longer store pickles in stoneware jars tied over with kid leather. Actually glass lids are preferable to metal ones for vinegar preserving; they won't corrode on long standing. In addition, the glass-topped relish or pickle makes a more attractive gift, visible from every angle.

Our mothers never bothered to treat their pickles and relishes with the boiling-water bath, but, properly done, it can prevent spoilage without overcooking the product. Time the bath carefully; the contents in the center of the jar need only reach 180° to inhibit the enzymes that cause spoilage.

Just bear in mind, as things come due for pickling, that Christmas is imminent and somebody has a birthday coming soon. Make a few more jars of each batch. Single persons, downtowners — anyone not in a position to make those delicious relishes themselves — all love being remembered on special days with a gift of made-in-your-kitchen pickles and relishes.

A mélange of condiments. Clockwise from rear: Sweet Cucumber Pickles, Tiny Pickled Onions, Corn Relish, Tomato Relish, Pickled Peaches, Hot Cranberry Chutney, Pickled Carrots, and Beet Pickles.

FRUIT AND VEGETABLE PICKLES

SPICED CRAB APPLES

1 (3-inch) stick cinnamon
1 tablespoon whole cloves
1 teaspoon whole allspice
2 quarts crab apples with
  stems
6 cups sugar
3 cups vinegar
3 cups water

Combine cinnamon, cloves, and allspice; tie loosely in a cheesecloth bag. Set aside.

Wash crab apples; drain well. Remove any blossoms. Pierce blossom end of each crab apple with a large sterilized needle to prevent skin from bursting. Set crab apples aside.

Combine sugar, vinegar, and water in a stainless steel stockpot, stirring well; add spice bag. Bring mixture to a boil; boil, stirring constantly, until syrup coats a metal spoon. Remove from heat, and let cool to room temperature.

Add reserved crab apples to syrup; reheat slowly over low heat to avoid bursting the skins. Simmer until crab apples are tender, stirring occasionally. Remove spice bag; discard.

Pack crab apples into hot sterilized jars, and cover with hot syrup, leaving ½-inch headspace. Remove air bubbles. Cover with metal lids, and screw bands tight. Process crab apples in boiling-water bath 20 minutes. Yield: 6 pints.

A 1910 postcard shows Florida grape harvest.

PICKLED FIGS

2 (3-inch) sticks cinnamon
1 tablespoon whole allspice
1 tablespoon whole cloves
5 cups sugar, divided
2 quarts water
4 quarts firm, ripe figs,
  peeled
3 cups vinegar

Combine cinnamon, allspice, and cloves; tie loosely in a cheesecloth bag. Set aside.

Combine 3 cups sugar and water in a stainless steel stockpot; cook over medium heat, stirring constantly, until sugar dissolves. Add figs; cook over low heat 30 minutes. Add remaining sugar, vinegar, and spice bag, mixing well. Cook over medium heat, stirring occasionally, until figs are clear.

Remove from heat; cover and let stand 12 to 24 hours in a cool place. Remove spice bag; discard. Slowly reheat fig mixture over low heat until thoroughly heated.

Pack figs into hot sterilized jars, leaving ½-inch headspace. Remove air bubbles. Cover at once with metal lids, and screw bands tight. Process figs in boiling-water bath 15 minutes. Yield: about 8 pints.

SPICED GRAPES

4 (3-inch) sticks cinnamon
1 (1.12-ounce) box whole
  cloves
1 teaspoon ground mace
8 pounds Concord grapes
3 cups cider vinegar
8 cups sugar

Combine cinnamon, cloves, and mace; tie loosely in a cheesecloth bag. Set aside.

Remove skins from grapes, reserving skins and pulp. Place pulp in a stainless steel stockpot; cook over medium-low heat, stirring frequently, until pulp is tender. Press through a sieve; discard seeds. Set pulp aside.

Combine spice bag, vinegar, and sugar in stockpot, stirring well; bring to a boil. Add reserved grape skins and pulp; return to a boil, stirring frequently. Reduce heat; simmer, stirring frequently, 1 hour or until mixture thickens. Remove spice bag; discard.

Quickly ladle mixture into hot sterilized jars, leaving ½-inch headspace. Remove air bubbles. Cover with metal lids, and screw bands tight. Process in boiling-water bath 10 minutes. Yield: 11 half pints.

SPICED MANGOS

2 tablespoons grated orange rind
2 tablespoons whole cloves
1 tablespoon whole allspice
3 (3-inch) sticks cinnamon
2 bay leaves, crushed
4 cups sugar
2 cups white vinegar
1 cup water
9 firm, ripe mangos (about 8 pounds), peeled and sliced

Combine first 5 ingredients; tie in a cheesecloth bag. Combine spice bag, sugar, vinegar, and water in a stainless steel stockpot. Bring to a boil. Add mangos. Reduce heat; simmer, stirring occasionally, 10 minutes or until fruit becomes translucent. Remove from heat; cool to room temperature. Cover and refrigerate overnight.

Bring mango mixture to a boil. Reduce heat; simmer, uncovered, 1 hour and 15 minutes, stirring frequently. Remove spice bag; discard.

Quickly pack mangos into hot sterilized jars, and cover with any remaining syrup, leaving ½-inch headspace. Remove air bubbles. Cover at once with metal lids, and screw bands tight. Process mangos in boiling-water bath 20 minutes. Yield: about 9 half pints.

What fun to be sent to the pantry around 1940!

PICKLED PEACHES

4 (2-inch) sticks cinnamon
2 tablespoons whole cloves, crushed
2 quarts water
1 tablespoon noniodized salt
1 tablespoon white vinegar
8 pounds firm, ripe small peaches
6 cups sugar
1 tablespoon ground ginger
1 quart white vinegar

Combine cinnamon and cloves; tie loosely in a cheese-cloth bag. Set aside.

Combine water, salt, and 1 tablespoon vinegar in a large glass mixing bowl; stir well.

Peel each peach, and immediately drop into acidulated water. Set aside.

Combine sugar, ginger, and vinegar in a stainless steel stockpot, stirring until sugar dissolves. Bring to a boil; boil 5 minutes. Add spice bag.

Drain peaches; rinse in cold water, and drain well. Carefully add to boiling syrup mixture. Boil until peaches are tender, but not soft. Remove from heat; cover and let stand in a cool place overnight, allowing peaches to plump. Remove spice bag; discard.

Return peach mixture to a boil; remove from heat. Quickly pack peaches into hot sterilized jars; cover with hot syrup, leaving ½-inch headspace. Remove air bubbles. Cover with metal lids, and screw bands tight. Process peaches in boiling-water bath 20 minutes. Yield: about 3 quarts.

Pickled Pears wear red for holiday "gifting." Spicy Pineapple Sticks repose in their syrup.

PICKLED PEARS

2 tablespoons mixed pickling spices
2 teaspoons whole cloves
2 (2-inch) pieces fresh gingerroot
1 lemon, thinly sliced
2 dozen firm, ripe pickling pears
6 cups sugar
1 quart white vinegar
1 quart water
½ cup red hot cinnamon candy (optional)

Combine pickling spices, cloves, gingerroot, and lemon; tie in a cheesecloth bag. Set aside.

Peel pears, leaving whole with stem intact. Set aside.

Combine spice bag, sugar, vinegar, water, and cinnamon candy, if desired, in a stainless steel stockpot. Bring to a boil. Reduce heat; simmer 5 minutes, stirring frequently. Add pears, a few at a time; simmer 15 minutes or just until tender. Remove from heat; cool pears in syrup to room temperature. Cover and refrigerate 12 to 18 hours. Remove spice bag; discard. Bring mixture to a boil.

Quickly pack pears into hot sterilized jars, and cover with syrup, leaving ½-inch headspace. Remove air bubbles. Cover with metal lids, and screw bands tight. Process pears in boiling-water bath 15 minutes. Yield: 5 quarts.

A Laurel, Delaware, watermelon shipment, c.1905.

SPICY PINEAPPLE STICKS

1 tablespoon whole cloves
2 teaspoons whole allspice
2 (3-inch) sticks cinnamon, broken
1 large lemon, sliced
4 cups sugar
2 cups white vinegar
2 large pineapples, peeled, cored, and cut into sticks

Combine first 4 ingredients; tie in a cheesecloth bag. Combine spice bag, sugar, and vinegar in a stainless steel stockpot. Bring to a boil. Add pineapple sticks. Reduce heat; simmer, stirring occasionally, 25 minutes or until pineapple is clear. Remove spice bag; discard.

Pack pineapple into hot sterilized jars, and cover with hot syrup, leaving ½-inch headspace. Remove air bubbles. Cover with metal lids, and screw bands tight. Process in boiling-water bath 10 minutes. Yield: 5 half pints.

PICKLED WATERMELON RIND

2 pounds watermelon rind (1 medium watermelon)
1 tablespoon pickling lime
7 cups water, divided
1 quart white vinegar, divided
3 (3-inch) sticks cinnamon
1 tablespoon whole cloves
1 tablespoon whole allspice
5 cups sugar

Remove outer green skin and pink flesh of watermelon rind. Cut greenish-white portion of rind into 1-inch cubes or other shapes, if desired.

Place rind in a large glass, ceramic, or stainless steel container. Combine lime and 1 quart cold water; pour over rind. Cover and let stand in a cool place 3 hours. Drain and rinse in 3 baths of cold water.

Place rind in a 10-quart stainless steel stockpot; cover with cold water. Bring to a boil, and boil slowly, stirring occasionally, 1 hour or until rind is translucent. Drain well.

Combine rind, 2 cups water, and 1 cup vinegar in a glass container; mix well. Cover and let stand in a cool place overnight. Drain; cover and set aside.

Combine cinnamon, cloves, and allspice; tie loosely in a cheesecloth bag. Combine spice bag, remaining 1 cup water, 3 cups vinegar, and sugar in stockpot. Bring to a boil; remove from heat. Cover and let stand 1 hour. Add rind to syrup. Bring to a boil; reduce heat, and cook over low heat, stirring occasionally, 2 hours or until rind is translucent. Remove spice bag; discard.

Pack rind into hot sterilized jars; pour syrup over pickles, leaving ½-inch headspace. Remove air bubbles. Cover with metal lids, and screw bands tight. Process watermelon rind in boiling-water bath 15 minutes. Yield: 3 pints.

A 1906 postcard with variations of the "beat it" theme. Beet Pickles are an "unbeatable" favorite.

JERUSALEM ARTICHOKE PICKLES

4 pounds Jerusalem artichokes, peeled and sliced
1 large white onion, peeled and sliced
½ cup salt
1 tablespoon plus 1½ teaspoons mustard seeds
1 tablespoon plus 1½ teaspoons whole peppercorns
1 tablespoon ground turmeric
2 teaspoons whole allspice
½ teaspoon whole cloves
2 (3-inch) sticks cinnamon, broken
1 quart white vinegar
1½ cups firmly packed brown sugar

Combine artichokes and onion in a large glass container; sprinkle with salt. Cover and refrigerate 24 hours. Rinse mixture several times in cold water; drain well.

Combine spices; tie loosely in a cheesecloth bag. Combine spice bag, vinegar, and sugar in a stainless steel stockpot. Bring to a boil; boil 3 minutes, stirring until sugar dissolves. Add artichoke mixture. Reduce heat; simmer 5 minutes, stirring frequently. Remove spice bag and onion; discard. Pack artichokes into hot sterilized jars, and cover with hot syrup, leaving ½-inch headspace. Remove air bubbles. Cover at once with metal lids, and screw bands tight. Process artichokes in boiling-water bath 10 minutes. Yield: 4½ pints.

DILLY BEANS

2 pounds green beans
1 teaspoon red pepper
4 cloves garlic
¼ cup plus 2 tablespoons dill seeds
2½ cups white vinegar
2½ cups water
¼ cup salt

Cut ends from beans; remove strings, if necessary. Pack beans vertically into 4 hot sterilized jars. Place ¼ teaspoon red pepper, 1 clove garlic, and 1½ tablespoons dill seeds in each of 4 jars.

Combine vinegar, water, and salt in a medium-size stainless steel saucepan; bring to a boil, and pour over beans, leaving ½-inch headspace. Remove air bubbles. Cover with metal lids, and screw bands tight. Process in boiling-water bath 10 minutes. Yield: 4 pints.

BEET PICKLES

5 pounds fresh beets
12 whole cloves
2 (3-inch) sticks cinnamon
2 bay leaves
2 sprigs fresh dill
2 cups cider vinegar
2 cups sugar
1 cup water

Leave root and 1 inch of stem on beets; scrub well. Place in a large stainless steel saucepan; add water to cover. Bring to a boil. Reduce heat; cover and simmer 35 minutes or until beets are tender. Drain. Cover with cold water; drain again. Let cool. Trim off stems and roots; rub off skins. Cut beets into ¼-inch-thick slices; pack into hot sterilized jars.

Combine spices, vinegar, sugar, and water in saucepan. Bring to a boil; boil 1 minute, stirring constantly. Strain syrup; discard spices.

Pour hot syrup over beets, leaving ½-inch headspace. Remove air bubbles. Cover with metal lids, and screw bands tight. Process in boiling-water bath 30 minutes. Yield: 5 pints.

PICKLED CARROTS

2 (12-ounce) packages baby carrots
1 tablespoon mixed pickling spices
1 (3-inch) stick cinnamon, broken
1 cup sugar
2 cups white vinegar
1½ cups water
1 teaspoon salt

Combine carrots and water to cover in a medium-size stainless steel saucepan. Bring to a boil. Reduce heat; cover and simmer 10 minutes or just until tender. Drain. Peel carrots; cut off stem end. Pack vertically into hot sterilized jars.

Combine spices; tie loosely in a cheesecloth bag. Combine spice bag, sugar, vinegar, water, and salt in saucepan. Bring to a boil; boil 8 minutes, stirring occasionally. Remove spice bag; discard. Pour hot syrup over carrots, leaving ½-inch headspace. Remove air bubbles. Cover with metal lids, and screw bands tight. Process in boiling-water bath 30 minutes. Yield: 3 half pints.

CAULIFLOWER PICKLES

3 quarts cauliflower flowerets (about 2 large heads)
1½ cups tiny pickling onions, peeled
¼ cup salt
2 tablespoons mustard seeds
1 tablespoon celery seeds
1 red pepper pod (optional)
1 teaspoon ground turmeric
1 quart white vinegar
2 cups sugar

Combine cauliflower, onions, and salt in a large glass container; cover with ice. Let stand 2 to 3 hours. Drain and rinse 3 times in a cold water bath.

Tie spices in a cheesecloth bag. Combine spice bag, vinegar, and sugar in a stainless steel stockpot. Bring to a boil. Add cauliflower and onions. Reduce heat; simmer 7 minutes, stirring occasionally. Remove spice bag; discard.

Pack cauliflower into hot sterilized jars; cover with syrup, leaving ½-inch headspace. Remove air bubbles. Cover with metal lids, and screw bands tight. Process in boiling-water bath 10 minutes. Yield: 4 pints.

Girls Canning Club demonstration at the Virginia State Fair. Photographed in 1914.

SWEET CUCUMBER RINGS

1 cup pickling lime
1 gallon water
7 pounds cucumbers, peeled, cored, and cut into ¼-inch slices
1 quart vinegar, divided
1 (1-ounce) bottle red food coloring
3 cups water
9 cups sugar
3 (5-ounce) packages red hot cinnamon candy
12 (3-inch) sticks cinnamon

Dissolve lime in 1 gallon water in a large glass, ceramic, or stainless steel container. Add cucumber slices. Cover and let stand 24 hours in a cool place.

Drain and rinse cucumbers 3 times in cold water. Cover cucumbers with ice; let stand 3 hours. Rinse and drain well.

Combine cucumbers, 1 cup vinegar, red food coloring, and water to cover in a stainless steel stockpot. Bring to a boil. Reduce heat; simmer, uncovered, 1 hour, stirring frequently. Drain well.

Combine remaining vinegar, 3 cups water, sugar, candy, and cinnamon in a large saucepan. Bring to a boil. Pour syrup over cucumbers. Cover and let stand at room temperature 24 hours. Discard cinnamon.

Bring cucumber mixture to a boil. Pack into hot sterilized jars; cover with syrup, leaving ½-inch headspace. Cover with metal lids, and screw bands tight. Process in boiling-water bath 10 minutes. Yield: 9 pints.

The popular pickle adds zest to any meal. Left to right: Dill Pickles, Sweet Cucumber Rings, and Bread and Butter Pickles.

SWEET CUCUMBER PICKLES

1 cup pickling lime
1 gallon water
7 pounds small, fresh cucumbers, cut into ⅛-inch slices
1 (1.25 ounce) can mixed pickling spices
10 cups sugar
2½ quarts vinegar

Dissolve lime in water in a large glass, ceramic, or stainless steel container. Add cucumber slices; cover and let stand in a cool place 24 hours. Drain and soak in cold water 4 hours, changing the water every hour. Drain and rinse well.

Tie pickling spices loosely in a cheesecloth bag. Combine spice bag, sugar, and vinegar in a stainless steel stockpot. Bring to a boil. Remove from heat; pour syrup over cucumbers. Cool. Cover and let stand in a cool place 24 hours or overnight. (Do not drain.)

Bring cucumber mixture to a boil. Reduce heat; simmer, uncovered, 25 minutes or until pickles are translucent, stirring frequently.

Pack pickles into hot sterilized jars; cover with syrup, leaving ½-inch headspace. Remove air bubbles. Cover at once with metal lids, and screw bands tight. Process in boiling-water bath 10 minutes. Yield: 12 pints.

BREAD AND BUTTER PICKLES

30 small cucumbers (about 5 pounds), cut into ⅛-inch slices
6 medium onions, thinly sliced
½ cup salt
1 quart vinegar
3 cups sugar
1 tablespoon plus 1 teaspoon celery seeds
2 teaspoons mustard seeds
2 teaspoons ground ginger
1 teaspoon ground turmeric

Layer cucumbers, onion, and salt in a large glass or ceramic container; cover with ice. Let stand 2 hours. Drain and rinse cucumbers and onion 3 times in cold water.

Combine remaining ingredients in a stainless steel stockpot. Bring to a boil; add cucumbers and onion. Reduce heat; simmer, stirring occasionally, 30 minutes or until cucumbers are translucent.

Pack pickles into hot sterilized jars; cover with syrup, leaving ½-inch headspace. Remove air bubbles. Cover at once with metal lids, and screw bands tight. Process in boiling-water bath 10 minutes. Yield: 8 pints.

DILL PICKLES

30 to 40 medium cucumbers, sliced lengthwise
7 sprigs fresh dill
3 tablespoons mixed whole pickling spices
¾ cup sugar
½ cup salt
1 quart vinegar
1 quart water

Pack cucumbers into hot sterilized jars, leaving ½-inch headspace. Place a dill sprig in each jar. Set aside.

Tie pickling spices loosely in a cheesecloth bag. Combine spice bag, sugar, salt, vinegar, and water in a large stainless steel saucepan. Bring to a boil. Reduce heat; simmer 15 minutes, stirring occasionally. Discard spice bag.

Pour syrup over cucumbers, leaving ½-inch headspace. Remove air bubbles. Cover with metal lids, and screw bands tight. Process in boiling-water bath 15 minutes. Yield 7 pints.

Note: Only garden-fresh cucumbers should be used.

DILL CHIPS

4 pounds medium
  cucumbers, cut into ¼-inch
  slices
14 sprigs fresh dill
3½ teaspoons mustard seeds,
  divided
14 whole peppercorns,
  divided
4½ cups water
4 cups white vinegar
¼ cup plus 2 tablespoons salt

Pack cucumbers into 7 hot
sterilized jars. Place 2 dill
sprigs, ½ teaspoon mustard
seeds, and 2 peppercorns into
each jar.

Combine water, vinegar, and
salt in a large stainless steel
saucepan; bring to a boil. Pour
over cucumbers, leaving ½-inch
headspace. Remove air bubbles.
Cover with metal lids, and screw
bands tight. Process in boiling-
water bath 15 minutes. Yield:
about 7 pints.

FRENCH PICKLES

1 bunch celery, cleaned and
  cut into 1-inch pieces
6 large green peppers, seeded
  and cut into 1-inch strips
6 large red peppers, seeded
  and cut into 1-inch strips
2 cups coarsely chopped
  onion
2 cups sugar
1 tablespoon plus 1½
  teaspoons mustard seeds
1 tablespoon plus 1½
  teaspoons celery seeds
1½ teaspoons salt
2 cups vinegar

Combine vegetables in a
stainless steel stockpot; cover
with boiling water. Let stand 5
minutes; drain. Repeat procedure; drain well. Add remaining
ingredients, stirring well. Bring
to a boil; boil 15 minutes, stirring frequently.

Pack pickle mixture into hot
sterilized jars; cover with syrup,
leaving ½-inch headspace. Remove air bubbles. Cover with
metal lids, and screw bands
tight. Process in boiling-water
bath 20 minutes. Yield: 4 pints.

Display from Ball Brothers' canning booklet, 1943.

TINY PICKLED
ONIONS

2 quarts tiny whole pickling
  onions, peeled
½ cup salt
7 small hot red peppers
7 bay leaves
1 quart white vinegar
1 cup sugar
2 tablespoons mustard seeds
1 tablespoon plus 1 teaspoon
  prepared horseradish

Place onions in a large glass or
ceramic container; sprinkle
with salt. Add water to cover.
Cover and let stand in a cool
place 12 hours. Drain and rinse
onions several times in cold
water.

Pack onions into 7 hot sterilized jars. Place 1 hot red pepper
and 1 bay leaf in each jar.

Combine vinegar, sugar,
mustard seeds, and horseradish
in a stainless steel stockpot.
Bring to a boil. Reduce heat;
simmer 15 minutes, stirring occasionally. Pour syrup over
onions, leaving ½-inch headspace. Remove air bubbles.
Cover with metal lids, and screw
bands tight. Process in boiling-
water bath 10 minutes. Yield: 7
half pints.

GREEN TOMATO PICKLES

1 gallon thinly sliced, unpeeled green tomatoes
1 quart thinly sliced onion
⅓ cup salt
1 tablespoon whole peppercorns
1 tablespoon mustard seeds
1 teaspoon whole allspice
1 teaspoon celery seeds
⅛ teaspoon red pepper
1 lemon, thinly sliced
3 cups white vinegar
3 cups firmly packed brown sugar

Combine tomatoes and onion in a large glass, ceramic, or stainless steel container; sprinkle with salt. Cover and let stand in a cool place overnight. Rinse tomatoes and onion several times in cold water; drain. Set aside.

Combine peppercorns, mustard seeds, allspice, celery seeds, red pepper, and lemon slices; tie loosely in a cheesecloth bag. Combine spice bag, vinegar, and sugar in a stainless steel stockpot; bring to a boil. Add reserved tomatoes and onion. Return to a boil. Reduce heat; simmer, uncovered, 10 minutes, stirring gently several times. Remove spice bag, and discard.

Pack tomatoes into hot sterilized jars; cover with syrup, leaving ½-inch headspace. Remove air bubbles. Cover with metal lids, and screw bands tight. Process in boiling-water bath for 10 minutes. Yield: 4 pints.

Large containers of pickles and jam dwarf a procession of cooks on this trade card, c.1890.

SQUASH PICKLES

2 quarts thinly sliced yellow squash
2 cups thinly sliced white onion
1 cup chopped green pepper
¼ cup salt
2½ cups cider vinegar
3 cups sugar
2 teaspoons celery seeds
2 teaspoons mustard seeds

Layer squash, onion, and green pepper in a large glass or ceramic container; sprinkle with salt. Cover and let stand 1 hour. Rinse squash mixture several times in cold water; drain well.

Combine vinegar, sugar, celery seeds, and mustard seeds in a stainless steel stockpot; bring to a boil. Add squash mixture. Reduce heat; simmer 10 minutes, stirring occasionally.

Pack squash and onion into hot sterilized jars; cover with syrup, leaving ½-inch headspace. Remove air bubbles. Cover at once with metal lids, and screw bands tight. Process in boiling-water bath 15 minutes. Yield: 3½ pints.

ZUCCHINI PICKLES

2 pounds zucchini, thinly sliced
2 small onions, thinly sliced
¼ cup salt
2 teaspoons mustard seeds
1 teaspoon celery seeds
3 cups cider vinegar
2 cups sugar
1 teaspoon ground turmeric

Layer zucchini, onion, and salt in a large glass container; add water to cover. Let stand 2 hours. Rinse and drain zucchini and onion 3 times.

Combine mustard seeds and celery seeds; tie in a cheesecloth bag. Combine spice bag, vinegar, sugar, and turmeric in a large stainless steel saucepan; bring to a boil. Add zucchini mixture. Remove from heat; let stand 2 hours. Bring mixture to a boil. Reduce heat; simmer 5 minutes, stirring gently. Discard spice bag.

Pack vegetables into hot sterilized jars; cover with hot syrup, leaving ½-inch headspace. Remove air bubbles. Cover at once with metal lids, and screw bands tight. Process zucchini in boiling-water bath 15 minutes. Yield: 3 pints.

Give a garden in a jar: Mixed Vegetable Pickles.

MIXED VEGETABLE PICKLES

- 1 quart sliced small cucumbers (1-inch slices)
- 2 cups sliced carrots (1½-inch slices)
- 2 cups sliced celery (1½-inch slices)
- 2 cups small whole pickling onions
- 2 sweet red peppers, cut into ½-inch strips
- 1 small cauliflower, broken into flowerets
- 1 cup salt
- 1 gallon cold water
- 6½ cups white vinegar
- 2 cups sugar
- 1 fresh hot red pepper, sliced crosswise
- ¼ cup mustard seeds
- 2 tablespoons celery seeds

Combine cucumber, carrot, celery, onions, sweet red pepper, and cauliflower in a large glass, ceramic, or stainless steel container. Dissolve salt in water; pour over vegetable mixture. Cover and let stand in a cool place 12 hours. Rinse and drain 3 times.

Combine vinegar, sugar, hot red pepper, and mustard and celery seeds in a stainless steel stockpot. Bring to a boil; boil 3 minutes, stirring until sugar dissolves. Add vegetables. Reduce heat; simmer, stirring gently several times, until thoroughly heated.

Pack vegetables into hot sterilized jars; cover with syrup, leaving ½-inch headspace. Remove air bubbles. Cover with metal lids, and screw bands tight. Process in boiling-water bath 15 minutes. Yield: 5 pints.

Note: The spices may be tied in a cheesecloth bag and discarded before packing into jars.

Southern cooks have always known that pickling is a frugal way to preserve the bounty of fruits and vegetables that come from a surplus harvest. Homemade pickles, relishes, and chutneys, in infinite combination, add flavor to salads or sauces. If pickle is absent when a platter of cold meat is being served, expect a polite request for a sweet-sour accompaniment. Served as part of a meal, a snack, or an hors d'oeuvre, the piquant delicacies add interest and variety to the palate. Mixed Vegetable Pickles reflect holiday colors.

FRUIT AND VEGETABLE RELISHES

GRAPE RELISH

4 pounds Concord grapes
4 cups sugar
⅔ cup cider vinegar
1 tablespoon ground
 cinnamon
1 teaspoon ground cloves

Wash and drain grapes; remove stems. Plunge grapes into rapidly boiling water; boil 2 minutes. Drain well, and slip off grape skins, reserving skins and pulp.

Place pulp in a stainless steel stockpot; bring to a boil. Reduce heat; simmer, uncovered, 20 minutes. Remove from heat. Process pulp through a food mill; discard seeds.

Combine sugar, vinegar, cinnamon, and cloves in Dutch oven; bring to a boil. Reduce heat to medium; add reserved hulls and pulp. Simmer, stirring occasionally, 1 hour and 45 minutes or until tender.

Quickly ladle relish into hot sterilized jars, leaving ½-inch headspace. Cover at once with metal lids, and screw bands tight. Process relish in boiling-water bath 15 minutes. Serve with meats. Yield: about 5 half pints.

A Tennessee child at the grape arbor, c.1940.

Pear Relish (left) and Peach Relish with pinked covers and ribbon. Happily, gift includes recipe!

PEAR RELISH

3½ pounds pears, peeled, cored, and coarsely chopped
1 quart sliced onion
6 medium-size dill pickles, cut into large pieces
4 green peppers, seeded and coarsely chopped
2 sweet red peppers, seeded and coarsely chopped
1 hot red pepper
2 tablespoons salt
2 cups sugar
2 tablespoons cornstarch
3 tablespoons dry mustard
1 tablespoon ground turmeric
1 quart cider vinegar

Grind together pears, onion, pickles, and peppers in a large mixing bowl, using coarse blade of a food grinder. Add salt, stirring well. Cover and let stand at room temperature 1 hour. Rinse and drain. Set aside.

Combine sugar, cornstarch, mustard, and turmeric in a stainless steel stockpot; stir well. Add vinegar, stirring to make a paste. Stir in reserved ground vegetables. Bring to a rolling boil. Reduce heat to medium; cook, uncovered, 50 minutes or until vegetables are tender and mixture thickens; stir frequently.

Quickly ladle relish into hot sterilized jars, leaving ½-inch headspace. Remove air bubbles. Cover with metal lids, and screw bands tight. Process relish in boiling-water bath 15 minutes. Serve with meats or vegetables. Yield: 5½ pints.

PEACH RELISH

2 quarts firm, sliced, peeled peaches
1½ cups firmly packed brown sugar
1 cup raisins
¾ cup cider vinegar
2 teaspoons mustard seeds
1 teaspoon ground cinnamon
½ teaspoon ground cloves
½ cup chopped pecans

Combine all ingredients, except pecans, in a stainless steel stockpot, stirring well. Bring to a boil. Reduce heat to medium, and cook, stirring frequently, 45 minutes or until mixture thickens. Stir in pecans, and cook 2 additional minutes.

Quickly ladle relish into hot sterilized jars, leaving ½-inch headspace. Remove air bubbles. Cover with metal lids, and screw bands tight. Process relish in boiling-water bath 15 minutes. Serve with meats. Yield: 5 half pints.

PEAR MINCEMEAT

7½ pounds pears, peeled and cored
4 pounds cooking apples, peeled and cored
2 pounds raisins
6 cups sugar
1 tablespoon ground cinnamon
½ cup cider vinegar
1 tablespoon whole nutmeg
1 tablespoon whole allspice

Grind together pears, apples, and raisins in a stainless steel stockpot, using coarse blade of a food grinder. Stir in sugar, cinnamon, and vinegar. Combine nutmeg and allspice; tie loosely in a cheesecloth bag. Add to fruit mixture. Cook over medium heat, stirring frequently, 1 hour or until mixture thickens.

Quickly ladle mincemeat into hot sterilized jars, leaving ½-inch headspace. Remove air bubbles. Cover with metal lids, and screw bands tight. Process in boiling-water bath 15 minutes. Serve as a condiment with cold meats and vegetables. Yield: about 10 pints.

In the South, it seems that if one has pears, one has too many pears, hence the multiplicity of ways we have learned to preserve them with both sugar and vinegar. We must be ever mindful of the Dixie dweller with no pears who stands in need of a gift of Pear Relish or Pear Mincemeat. Attach a serving suggestion: "Serve on crackers with thinly sliced ham." Add a jar of Pear Honey (page 27) with a partridge-shaped label.

"Earliest" is obviously better on this seeds ad, c.1900.

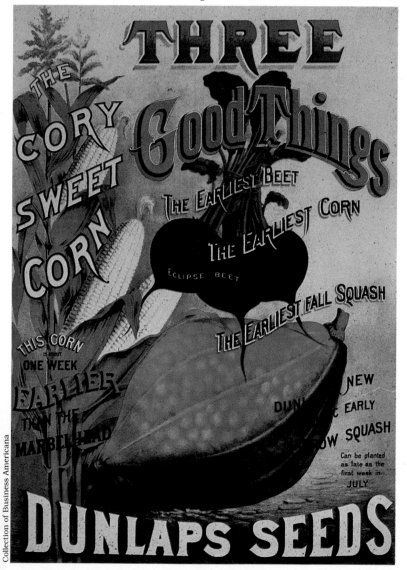

CORN RELISH

About 18 ears fresh corn
7 quarts water
1 small head cabbage, chopped
1 cup chopped onion
1 cup chopped, seeded green pepper
1 cup chopped, seeded sweet red pepper
1 to 2 cups sugar
2 tablespoons dry mustard
1 tablespoon celery seeds
1 tablespoon mustard seeds
1 tablespoon salt
1 tablespoon ground turmeric
1 quart white vinegar
1 cup water

Remove husks and silk from corn just before cooking. Bring 7 quarts water to a boil in a stainless steel stockpot; add corn. Return to a boil; boil 5 minutes. Drain.

Cut corn from cob to measure about 2 quarts. Combine corn kernels and remaining ingredients in stockpot. Bring to a boil. Reduce heat; simmer, uncovered, 20 minutes, stirring frequently.

Quickly ladle relish into hot sterilized jars, leaving ½-inch headspace. Remove air bubbles. Cover with metal lids, and screw bands tight. Process in boiling-water bath 15 minutes. Yield: 8 half pints.

CARROT RELISH

5 cups unpeeled, ground green tomatoes
3 cups ground cabbage
1½ cups ground onion
1½ cups ground cucumbers
1½ cups ground carrots
1 medium-size green pepper, seeded and ground
1 medium-size sweet red pepper, seeded and ground
¼ cup salt
4½ cups cider vinegar
2⅓ cups firmly packed brown sugar
¼ cup celery seeds
¼ cup mustard seeds
1 teaspoon red pepper

Combine ground vegetables and salt in a large glass mixing bowl, stirring well; cover and refrigerate 4 hours. Rinse in cold water, and drain.

Combine vegetables, vinegar, sugar, celery and mustard seeds, and red pepper in a large non-aluminum stockpot, stirring well; bring to a boil. Reduce heat; simmer, uncovered, 20 minutes or until vegetables are tender, stirring frequently.

Quickly ladle relish into hot sterilized jars, leaving ½-inch headspace. Remove air bubbles. Cover with metal lids, and screw bands tight. Process in boiling-water bath 10 minutes. Serve with meats or vegetables. Yield: about 10 pints.

RED PEPPER RELISH

12 medium-size sweet red peppers, seeded and ground
¼ cup salt
3 cups sugar
2 cups cider vinegar

Combine ground peppers and salt in a large glass, ceramic, or stainless steel container, stirring well; cover and refrigerate 2 hours. Drain. Rinse with cold water, and drain well.

Combine pepper, sugar, and

CUCUMBER RELISH

1 quart ground, unpeeled cucumber
3 cups finely diced celery
3 cups ground onion
1 cup seeded and ground green pepper
½ cup seeded and ground sweet red pepper
¼ cup salt
3½ cups sugar
2 cups cider vinegar
1 tablespoon whole mustard seeds
2 teaspoons celery seeds

Combine first 5 ingredients in a large glass mixing bowl; add salt, mixing well. Add water to cover. Cover and let stand in a cool place overnight. Rinse and drain well. Set aside.

Combine sugar, vinegar, and mustard and celery seeds in a stainless steel stockpot; bring to a boil, stirring until sugar dissolves. Add vegetable mixture. Reduce heat; simmer, uncovered, 30 minutes or until vegetables are tender, stirring frequently.

Quickly ladle relish into hot sterilized jars, leaving ½-inch headspace. Remove air bubbles. Cover with metal lids, and screw bands tight. Process in boiling-water bath 10 minutes. Serve with meats or vegetables. Yield: 4 pints.

vinegar in a stainless steel stockpot, stirring well; bring to a boil. Boil until mixture thickens.

Ladle relish into hot sterilized jars, leaving ½-inch headspace. Remove air bubbles. Cover at once with metal lids, and screw bands tight. Process relish in boiling-water bath 10 minutes. Serve with meats and vegetables. Yield: 2½ pints.

PEPPER HASH

15 medium onions, ground
12 medium-size green peppers, seeded and ground
12 large sweet red peppers, seeded and ground
1 quart plus 2⅔ cups cider vinegar, divided
1⅓ cups water
2 cups sugar
3 tablespoons mustard seeds
1 tablespoon celery seeds
3 tablespoons salt

Combine onion and peppers in a large glass, ceramic, or stainless steel container. Cover with boiling water; let stand 10 minutes. Drain thoroughly.

Combine 2⅔ cups vinegar and water in a medium-size stainless steel saucepan; bring to a boil. Pour over pepper mixture; let stand 10 minutes. Drain thoroughly.

Combine remaining vinegar, sugar, mustard and celery seeds, and salt in saucepan; bring to a boil. Add drained pepper mixture; simmer 2 hours or until onions are translucent, stirring frequently.

Pack hash into hot sterilized jars, leaving ½-inch headspace. Remove air bubbles. Cover with metal lids, and screw bands tight. Process in boiling-water bath 20 minutes. Serve with meats or vegetables. Yield: 8 pints.

Red Pepper Relish (front) and Squash Relish (page 52) will be received with delight. Patchwork covers dress the jars.

SQUASH RELISH

3 quarts water
⅔ cup salt
2 quarts chopped yellow
  squash
3 cups sugar
2 cups white vinegar
1 to 1½ tablespoons celery
  seeds
1½ tablespoons mustard
  seeds
2 cups chopped onion
2 cups chopped, seeded green
  pepper
3 green onions, chopped
1 (4-ounce) jar sliced
  pimientos, drained

Combine water and salt in a large glass, ceramic, or stainless steel container. Add squash and soak 1 hour. Drain squash, and rinse well.

Combine sugar, vinegar, and celery and mustard seeds in a stainless steel stockpot; stir well. Bring to a boil. Add squash and remaining ingredients. Return to a rolling boil; reduce heat, and cook 5 minutes, stirring frequently.

Quickly ladle relish into hot sterilized jars, leaving ½-inch headspace. Remove air bubbles. Cover with metal lids, and screw bands tight. Process relish in boiling water-bath 15 minutes. Serve with meats and vegetables. Yield: about 4 pints.

GREEN TOMATO MINCEMEAT

3 pounds (about 9) small
  green tomatoes, cored and
  chopped
3 cups water, divided
3 pounds tart green apples,
  peeled, cored, and chopped
2 (15-ounce) packages
  seedless raisins
4 (16-ounce) packages brown
  sugar
1 cup cider vinegar
3 tablespoons grated orange
  rind
2 tablespoons salt
2 tablespoons ground
  cloves
1 tablespoon ground
  cinnamon
1 tablespoon ground nutmeg

Combine tomatoes and 1 cup water in a stainless steel stockpot. Bring to a boil. Drain well. Add 1 cup water; return to a boil. Drain well. Add 1 cup water; return to boil. Remove from heat, and drain tomatoes.

Combine tomatoes and remaining ingredients in stockpot. Bring to a boil. Reduce heat, and simmer, uncovered, 1 hour or until mixture thickens, stirring frequently.

Quickly ladle mincemeat into hot sterilized jars, leaving ½-inch headspace. Remove air bubbles. Cover with metal lids, and screw bands tight. Process in boiling-water bath 25 minutes. Yield: 7½ pints.

Note: For a mincemeat pie, combine 1 quart mincemeat, 1 chopped, peeled apple, and 1 tablespoon butter; mix well. Bake as any mincemeat pie.

GREEN TOMATO CHOW CHOW

4 quarts (about 24 large)
  sliced green tomatoes
½ cup salt
1 large head cabbage, cored
  and shredded
1 pound sweet red peppers,
  seeded and finely chopped
1 pound onions, finely
  chopped
1 hot red pepper, finely
  chopped
1 cup firmly packed brown
  sugar
2 tablespoons mustard seeds
1 tablespoon celery seeds
1 tablespoon whole cloves
1 tablespoon ground allspice
2 teaspoons dry mustard
3 pints vinegar

Combine tomatoes and salt in a large glass, ceramic, or stainless steel container. Cover and let stand overnight; drain. Rinse and drain in 2 baths of cold water. Soak tomatoes in cold water to cover 30 minutes; drain.

Grind tomatoes into a stainless steel stockpot, using coarse blade of a meat grinder. Stir in remaining ingredients, and cook, uncovered, over medium-high heat 1 hour, stirring occasionally to prevent sticking.

Quickly ladle chow chow into hot sterilized jars, leaving ½-inch headspace. Remove air bubbles. Cover at once with metal lids, and screw bands tight. Process chow chow in boiling-water bath 15 minutes. Yield: 2 quarts.

TOMATO RELISH

12 medium tomatoes peeled,
   cored, and coarsely chopped
¾ cup chopped onion
4 fresh hot green peppers,
  seeded and chopped
½ cup white vinegar
½ cup firmly packed brown
  sugar
1 teaspoon salt
½ teaspoon pepper
¼ teaspoon ground cinnamon
¼ teaspoon ground cloves
¼ teaspoon ground allspice

Combine all ingredients in a stainless steel stockpot, stirring well. Bring mixture to a boil. Reduce heat; simmer, uncovered, until mixture thickens, stirring occasionally.

Quickly ladle relish into hot sterilized jars, leaving ½-inch headspace. Remove air bubbles. Cover with metal lids, and screw bands tight. Process in boiling-water bath 15 minutes. Yield: about 4 half pints.

PICCALILLI

3 pounds (about 9) ripe red tomatoes, peeled and cored
3 pounds green tomatoes, cored
2 medium-size green peppers, seeded
2 sweet red peppers, seeded
1½ cups coarsely chopped celery
1 cup coarsely chopped onion
⅓ cup salt
1 quart cider vinegar
3 cups sugar
1 tablespoon ground cinnamon
1 tablespoon mustard seeds
1½ teaspoons whole cloves

Grind tomatoes, peppers, celery, and onion in a large glass mixing bowl, using coarse blade of a food grinder. Sprinkle with salt. Cover and let stand in a cool place overnight. Rinse several times in cold water; drain thoroughly.

Combine vegetable mixture and remaining ingredients in a stainless steel saucepan. Bring to a rolling boil. Reduce heat; simmer, uncovered, 1 hour, stirring frequently.

Pack mixture into hot sterilized jars, leaving ½-inch headspace. Remove air bubbles. Cover with metal lids, and screw bands tight. Process in boiling-water bath for 15 minutes. Serve with vegetables. Yield: 4 half pints.

Where is the poet sing the glories of the tomato, unsurpassed in usefulness and beauty, both fresh and preserved? From the first garden tomato of the season through a summer of tomato salads and "BLTs" to the final clearing out of the patch to make a Southern-style relish, let's spare a sigh for ages past when people thought tomatoes poisonous and grew them for their beauty alone.

A canning party in Guilford County, North Carolina, 1911.

SUMMER VEGETABLE RELISH

2 cups sliced cucumbers
2 cups chopped cabbage
2 cups chopped, seeded green pepper
2 cups chopped green tomato
2 cups chopped onion
2 quarts water
½ cup salt
2 cups chopped carrot
2 cups chopped cauliflower
2 cups chopped celery
2 cups cut green beans
2 cups chopped chayote squash
1 quart cider vinegar
4 cups sugar
2 cups water
¼ cup mustard seeds
2 tablespoons celery seeds
2 tablespoons ground turmeric

Combine first 7 ingredients in a large glass or ceramic container. Cover and refrigerate overnight. Drain and rinse in 3 cold water baths.

Combine carrot, cauliflower, celery, green beans, squash, and water to cover in a large stainless steel saucepan. Bring to a boil. Reduce heat; cover and simmer 15 minutes, stirring frequently. Drain well.

Combine vinegar, sugar, 2 cups water, and spices in a stainless steel stockpot; stir well. Bring to a boil. Add reserved vegetable mixtures, mixing well. Return to a boil. Reduce heat; simmer 10 minutes, stirring frequently.

Pack relish into hot sterilized jars, leaving ½-inch headspace. Remove air bubbles. Cover at once with metal lids, and screw bands tight. Process in boiling-water bath 10 minutes. Yield: 9 pints.

Aunt Fanny's Garden, an oil on panel, by Texas folk artist Clara McDonald Williamson, 1953.

To this point, you've been putting by pickles and relishes; you see chutneys coming. "Where," you ask, "are the pickled nasturtium seeds?" You have an abundance of the blossoms, which you love to use in the salad bowl as well as in bouquets. And you know the pods, pickled, are used like capers. Boil a cup of vinegar with a teaspoon of salt and a tiny spice bag. Refrigerate in a covered pint jar; drop pods in as the flowers are used. Fun to give!

APPLE CHUTNEY

2 quarts unpeeled, cored, and
  diced cooking apples
2 cups raisins, chopped
1 cup chopped pecans
Grated rind of 2 oranges
4 cups sugar
½ cup cider vinegar
½ teaspoon ground
  cloves

Combine all ingredients in a stainless steel stockpot; bring to a boil, stirring frequently. Reduce heat; simmer, uncovered, 2 hours or until mixture thickens, stirring frequently.

Quickly ladle chutney into hot sterilized jars, leaving ½-inch headspace. Remove air bubbles. Cover at once with metal lids, and screw bands tight. Process chutney in boiling-water bath 15 minutes. Yield: 12 half pints.

HOT CRANBERRY CHUTNEY

1 cup sugar
1 cup water
2 cups cranberries
½ cup raisins
¼ cup finely chopped
  almonds
2 tablespoons cider
  vinegar
1 tablespoon brown sugar
¼ teaspoon ground ginger
¼ teaspoon crushed red
  pepper

Combine sugar and water in a large stainless steel saucepan; bring to a boil. Boil, stirring constantly, until sugar dissolves. Reduce heat; add remaining ingredients. Continue to cook, uncovered, 10 minutes or until cranberries burst and mixture thickens, stirring occasionally. Remove from heat.

Quickly ladle chutney into hot sterilized jars, leaving ½-inch headspace. Remove air bubbles. Cover at once with metal lids, and screw bands tight. Process in boiling-water bath 15 minutes. Yield: about 3 half pints.

SEASONED GREETINGS

Who has the better of the bargain, the herb grower or the cook on the herb grower's gift list? The pleasure, I'm sure, is mutual. Herb culture is a happy, sharing hobby, and to have bottles of fines herbes and packets of bouquet garni in the kitchen helps us all to bring out the best in our cooking. Somehow, in making a nation out of a colony, we stopped pronouncing the *h* in herbs, possibly influenced by the cockney dialect among the early comers. But those 'erbs, carefully dried and bottled airtight, are important in Southern cuisine. Herb fanciers dry the branches covered with mosquito netting and hung upside down. The leaves are then picked whole and put into widemouthed jars, to be crushed at the moment of use.

Nongardeners will want to turn straight to the flavored sugars and salts for some gift ideas. Again, storage containers must be airtight. Ideal are commercial spice bottles that have both shaker tops and screw-on lids. With the old labels soaked off and your own brand in place, they are ready to be filled and beribboned for giving.

Making the variety of catsups and chili sauces in this chapter will inspire the vegetable gardener to an excess of Christmas generosity. He who goes in for hot pepper mixtures will need a word of caution. Down in the St. Augustine area, they put on rubber gloves to make "Bottled Hell" or Datil Pepper Vinegar. The Datil peppers are grown from seeds which originated from those brought by the Minorcans in 1777. Tiny bottles are required.

Gift vinegars are fun to make, and who could fail to be charmed with a bottle of Violet Vinegar or perhaps Mint Vinegar? With small containers, it is easy to put together sets of condiments for our friends. Mustards are high on the gourmet's list; be sure to include at least one. Vinegars and mustards can be made any time of the year, independent of any gardening skill or heavy investment of time.

The week before Christmas could find the confessed last-minute activator happily stirring up giftworthy jars of Beet-Horseradish or Cranberry-Orange relishes to tuck into friends' refrigerators when hopping from one holiday party to another. People and gifts: it takes all kinds.

Clockwise from Sweet Hot Mustard (front): Apple Catsup, Sauerkraut Relish, Barbecue Sauce, and Cranberry-Orange Relish. Each says "Greetings" tastefully.

SUGAR, SALT, AND HERB BLENDS

CINNAMON SUGAR

2 cups sugar
⅓ cup ground cinnamon

Combine sugar and cinnamon in a small mixing bowl; mix well. Store in airtight containers. Use to sprinkle on buttered toast or sugar cookies. Yield: 2⅓ cups.

VANILLA SUGAR

2 vanilla beans, cut into
  ½-inch pieces
2 cups sugar

Place vanilla beans in container of an electric blender, and process until powdered. Add sugar; process until mixture is fine. Store in airtight containers. Serve in coffee or over fresh fruit. Yield: 2 cups.

ORANGE-SPICE SUGAR

1 cup sugar
1 tablespoon grated orange
  rind
½ teaspoon ground
  cinnamon
¼ teaspoon ground nutmeg
¼ teaspoon ground
  cardamom
⅛ teaspoon ground ginger

Combine all ingredients in an 8-inch square baking dish. Bake at 200° for 15 minutes, stirring occasionally. Remove from oven, and cool completely.

Place mixture in container of an electric blender, and process until sugar is fine. Store in an airtight container. Serve in coffee or applesauce, or sprinkle on fresh apples, pancakes, waffles, or French toast. Yield: 1 cup.

LEMON-MINT SUGAR

1 cup sugar
1 tablespoon grated lemon
  or lime rind
1 tablespoon dried
  mint leaves
⅛ teaspoon salt

Combine sugar, grated rind, mint, and salt in an 8-inch square baking dish. Bake at 200° for 15 minutes, stirring occasionally. Remove from oven, and cool completely in pan.

Place mixture in container of an electric blender, and process until sugar is fine. Store in an airtight container. Serve in tea or punch, or sprinkle on fresh fruit. Yield: about 1 cup.

Clockwise from center: Lemon-Mint, Vanilla and Orange-Spice Sugars. Colored Sugar and Mold (page 64).

Cutting sugar cane in Louisiana, c.1890.

SUGAR REFINING

Conveyer belt being loaded.

Cane-crushing mill.

Tending the centrifugal processor.

Sugar mill in the Teche country of Louisiana.

Collection of pressed glass salt dishes, c. 1840, elaborately shaped; paddleboat (front right) is unique.

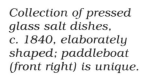

COLORED SUGAR MOLD

3 cups sugar
½ cup colored coarse sugar
1 tablespoon water

Combine all ingredients in a small mixing bowl; stir until dry ingredients are moistened. Press mixture firmly into an ungreased 3-cup mold. Let stand at least 30 minutes. Unmold and place in an airtight container. Break pieces from mold, and serve in tea or coffee. Yield: one 3-cup mold.

FRESH HERB SALT

¼ cup chopped fresh parsley
¼ cup fresh dill sprigs
¼ cup fresh tarragon leaves
½ cup salt
1 teaspoon paprika

Place parsley, dill, and tarragon on a baking sheet. Bake at 200° for 40 minutes or until herbs are dry. Crush herbs to a fine powder, using a mortar and pestle.

Combine powdered herbs, salt, and paprika in a small mixing bowl; stir well. Store in an airtight container. Use as a seasoning in poultry, fish, or vegetable dishes. Yield: ¾ cup.

SEASONED SALT

1 cup pickling salt
2½ teaspoons paprika
2 teaspoons dry mustard
1½ teaspoons dried whole oregano, crushed
1½ teaspoons garlic powder
1 teaspoon curry powder
1 teaspoon dried whole thyme, crushed
½ teaspoon onion powder
¼ teaspoon dried whole dillweed

Combine all ingredients in a small mixing bowl, mixing well. Store in an airtight container. Use as a seasoning in egg, cheese, fish, or meat dishes. Yield: 1¼ cups.

SEASONED SALT GALORE

1 (26-ounce) box iodized salt
⅓ cup garlic salt
¼ cup plus 1½ teaspoons onion salt
¼ cup plus ¾ teaspoon celery salt
¼ cup dried parsley flakes
2 tablespoons paprika
1 tablespoon plus 1½ teaspoons chili powder
1 tablespoon sugar
1 teaspoon pepper

Combine all ingredients in a medium mixing bowl, mixing well. Store in airtight containers. Use as a seasoning in meat, fish, poultry, or vegetable dishes. Yield: 4 cups.

KITCHEN SPICE

2 tablespoons salt
1 tablespoon dried lemon peel
1 tablespoon dry mustard
2 teaspoons ground allspice
2 teaspoons ground ginger
2 teaspoons ground nutmeg
2 teaspoons pepper
2 teaspoons red pepper

Combine all ingredients in a small mixing bowl, mixing well. Store in an airtight container.

Rub on roasts, lamb, veal, spareribs, or other meats. Allow 2 teaspoons for a 4-pound roast; ¼ teaspoon for a 1-pound cutlet. Add 1 teaspoon to a large pot of beef soup. Add ¼ teaspoon to 1 cup of meat or vegetable gravy. Yield: ½ cup.

How many of us rush to buy the herb and spice blends made according to "the secret recipes" of admired celebrities? We can read that label and nigh duplicate it. Remember: in commercial labeling, the proportion of ingredients is indicated by the order listed. If it contains more salt than anything else, salt is listed first, and so on. Why not market your own famous seafood seasoning or unparalleled salad dressing mix in the guise of a gift?

Salt exhibit at the Tri-State Fair, Memphis, 1934.

HERBES AROMATIQUES

2 cups kosher salt
15 large cloves garlic, peeled and cut in half
2 tablespoons paprika
1 tablespoon plus 1½ teaspoons poultry seasoning
1 tablespoon basil leaves
1 tablespoon celery seeds
1 tablespoon chili powder
1 tablespoon ground ginger
1 tablespoon onion powder
1 tablespoon dried whole oregano
1 teaspoon ground coriander
1 teaspoon ground cumin

Place salt in container of an electric blender; add garlic while processing at high speed. Add remaining ingredients; process until well blended. Store in airtight containers. Use in vegetables or salads. Yield: 3 cups.

DRIED HERB MIX

8 (.25-ounce) cans dried parsley flakes
5 (.37-ounce) jars dried marjoram leaves
3 (.75-ounce) jars dried whole thyme
3 (.75-ounce) jars dried savory
2 (.49-ounce) jars dried basil leaves
1 (1.3-ounce) jar dried lemon peel
1 teaspoon celery seeds
6 bay leaves, crushed

Combine all ingredients in a large mixing bowl; stir well. Spoon one-fourth of mixture into container of an electric blender; process until coarsely ground. Repeat procedure with remaining herb mixture, processing one-fourth of mixture at a time. Store in airtight jars. Use as a seasoning in gravies, soups, or stews. Yield: 6 cups.

BOUQUETS GARNIS

24 small sprigs fresh parsley, divided
12 bay leaves, divided
1½ teaspoons dried whole thyme, divided
1½ teaspoons dried tarragon leaves, divided

Wrap 2 parsley sprigs, 1 bay leaf, ⅛ teaspoon thyme, and ⅛ teaspoon tarragon in each of twelve 6-inch squares of cheesecloth. Tie into a bag, using white string. Pack herb bouquets into a widemouthed jar with clamped lid. Yield: 1 dozen.

Note: Use as a seasoning for stews or sauces. Add Bouquet Garni for last 30 minutes of cooking.

Herbes Aromatiques (left) and Bouquets Garnis: make-ahead gifts for the serious cook.

CREOLE SEASONING

1 (26-ounce) box iodized salt
1 (2-ounce) can black pepper
1 (1½-ounce) can chili powder
1 (1½-ounce) can red pepper
1 (1-ounce) can garlic powder

Combine all ingredients in a medium mixing bowl; mix well. Store in airtight containers. Use as a seasoning in Creole recipes, fried chicken, or gravies. Yield: about 4 cups.

SAVORY ACCOMPANIMENTS

BASIL VINEGAR

9 fresh basil leaves
1 quart apple cider vinegar

Wash basil leaves thoroughly; let dry, and place in a sterilized widemouthed jar. Bruise leaves, using the back of a spoon.

Place vinegar in a medium saucepan; bring to a boil. Pour over leaves in jar. Cover with a metal lid, and screw band tight. Let stand 10 days; shake jar daily. Strain vinegar through 4 layers of cheesecloth into a decorative bottle, discarding herb residue. Seal with a cork or other airtight lid. Yield: 1 quart.

Note: If a stronger flavor is desired, add bruised basil leaves to strained vinegar, and allow to stand several more days.

GARLIC-CHIVE VINEGAR

10 to 12 cloves garlic
8 to 10 fresh chive leaves
1 quart white vinegar
Additional cloves garlic
Additional fresh chive leaves

Arrange 10 to 12 garlic cloves on 3 wooden skewers. Place skewers and chives in a widemouthed jar. Pour vinegar over herbs. Cover with a metal lid, and screw band tight. Let stand at room temperature 2 weeks.

Strain vinegar through 4 layers of cheesecloth into a tall decorative bottle. Discard herb residue; add additional garlic and chives. Seal with a cork or other airtight lid. Yield: about 1 quart.

MIXED HERB VINEGAR

3 sprigs fresh basil
3 sprigs fresh tarragon
6 sprigs fresh thyme
1 quart boiling vinegar

Wash herbs; arrange in a sterilized widemouthed jar. Bruise leaves and stems, using a wooden spoon. Pour hot vinegar over leaves in jar. Cover with a metal lid, and screw band tight. Let stand 10 days at room temperature; shake jar daily.

Strain vinegar through 4 layers of cheesecloth into a decorative bottle; discard herbs. Seal with a cork or other airtight lid. Use mixed herb vinegar in sauces and salad dressings. Yield: 1 quart.

TARRAGON WINE VINEGAR

3 sprigs fresh tarragon
3 sprigs fresh lemon balm
1 quart white wine
   vinegar
Additional tarragon

Wash herbs thoroughly; let dry, and place in a sterilized widemouthed jar. Bruise herbs, using a pestle or the back of a spoon.

Place vinegar in a medium saucepan; bring to a boil. Pour vinegar over herbs in jar. Cover with a metal lid, and screw band tight. Let stand 10 days in a warm place; shake jar daily.

Strain vinegar through 4 layers of cheesecloth into a decorative bottle, discarding herb residue. Add additional sprigs of tarragon. Seal bottle with a cork or other airtight lid. Yield: 1 quart.

Color plate of apples taken from The Orchard and Fruit Garden, *published in 1839.*

RED WINE VINEGAR

1 pint Burgundy or other dry
   red wine
1 pint apple cider vinegar
2 cloves garlic, minced
1 sprig fresh tarragon
3 whole peppercorns
Pinch of dried whole thyme

Combine all ingredients in a sterilized widemouthed jar. Cover with a metal lid, and screw band tight. Let stand several weeks.

Strain vinegar through 4 layers of cheesecloth into a decorative bottle, discarding residue. Seal with a cork or other airtight lid. Yield: 1 quart.

VIOLET VINEGAR

4 cups fresh wild violet
   blossoms
1 quart vinegar

Wash violets; let dry, and place in a sterilized jar.

Place vinegar in a medium-size saucepan; bring to a boil. Pour over violets in jar. Cover with a metal lid, and screw band tight. Let stand 5 days in a warm place; shake jar daily.

Strain vinegar through 4 layers of cheesecloth into a decorative bottle, discarding violets. Seal with a cork or other airtight lid. Use in salad dressings. Yield: 1 quart.

DATIL PEPPER VINEGAR

2 quarts datil peppers
1 clove garlic
3 tablespoons salt
2 (750 ml) bottles sherry

Grind peppers and garlic in a crock, using coarse blade of a meat grinder. Stir in salt and sherry. Cover and let stand at room temperature at least 2 months.

Strain pepper mixture through 4 layers of cheesecloth into decorative bottles; discard pepper. Seal bottles with corks or other airtight lids. Yield: about 3 quarts.

MINT VINEGAR

6 sprigs fresh mint
1 quart white wine vinegar

Wash mint; place in a sterilized widemouthed jar. Bruise mint leaves, using a wooden spoon. Pour vinegar over sprigs in jar. Cover with a metal lid, and screw band tight. Let stand 10 days; shake jar daily.

Strain vinegar through 4 layers of cheesecloth into a decorative bottle, discarding mint residue. Seal with a cork or other airtight lid. Use in meat sauces and salad dressings. Yield: 1 quart.

CHILE PEPPER VINEGAR

25 red chile peppers
25 green chile peppers
1⅓ cups white wine vinegar

Cut red and green chile peppers in half crosswise; place in a hot sterilized jar.

Place vinegar in a medium saucepan; bring to a boil. Pour over peppers in jar. Cover with a metal lid, and screw band tight. Refrigerate 2 weeks.

Pour vinegar into a decorative bottle; add chile peppers. Seal with a cork or other airtight lid. Yield: 1 quart.

Cover of musical "oddity" written by Adaline Shepherd.

Chile Pepper Vinegar (front) and Basil Vinegar in decorative containers.

TOMATO CATSUP

1 gallon finely chopped, peeled tomatoes
½ cup finely chopped onion
½ cup finely chopped green pepper
1½ cups sugar
1 tablespoon plus 1½ teaspoons ground cinnamon
1 tablespoon salt
1 tablespoon ground cloves
1 teaspoon ground ginger
½ cup vinegar

Combine all ingredients in a large stockpot; bring to a boil, stirring frequently. Continue to boil, uncovered, 2 hours, stirring occasionally. Press tomato mixture through a sieve; return strained mixture to stockpot. Bring to a boil. Boil gently 2 hours, stirring occasionally.

Quickly ladle catsup into hot sterilized jars, leaving ¼-inch headspace. Cover with metal lids, and screw bands tight. Process catsup in boiling-water bath 20 minutes. Yield: 3 pints.

TOMATO SAUCE

5 pounds ripe tomatoes, peeled, cored, and chopped
2 medium onions, finely chopped
2 cloves garlic, minced
1 bay leaf
1½ teaspoons salt
¾ teaspoon dried whole oregano
½ teaspoon pepper
⅛ teaspoon crushed red pepper
½ teaspoon sugar

Combine all ingredients in a large saucepan. Bring to a boil. Reduce heat; simmer 2 hours, stirring occasionally. Press mixture through a food mill. Return mixture to saucepan. Cook over medium heat, stirring frequently, 25 minutes or until thickened.

Pour into hot sterilized jars, leaving ¼-inch headspace. Cover with metal lids; screw bands tight. Process in boiling-water bath 35 minutes. Yield: 4 half pints.

Put zest in your hot dogs with homemade Tomato Catsup.

APPLE CATSUP

12 medium cooking apples, peeled, cored, and quartered
2 cups water
1 medium onion, finely chopped
1 cup sugar
2 tablespoons ground cinnamon
1 tablespoon salt
1 tablespoon dry mustard
1 tablespoon ground cloves
1 tablespoon pepper
2 cups vinegar

Place apples and water in a large Dutch oven; cook over medium heat, stirring occasionally, until apples are soft. Press apples through a sieve. Discard cooking liquid.

Combine strained apple pulp and remaining ingredients in Dutch oven; bring to a boil. Boil, stirring frequently, 1 hour or until thickened.

Ladle catsup into hot sterilized jars, leaving ¼-inch headspace. Cover with metal lids, and screw bands tight. Process catsup in boiling-water bath 20 minutes. Yield: 4 pints.

CHILI SAUCE

12 large tomatoes, peeled and finely chopped
4 medium onions, finely chopped
3 large green peppers, seeded and finely chopped
2 cloves garlic, minced
½ cup sugar
2 tablespoons salt
1 teaspoon celery seeds
1 teaspoon ground cinnamon
1 teaspoon grated fresh nutmeg
1 teaspoon ground allspice
½ teaspoon ground cloves
¼ teaspoon red pepper
1 cup apple cider vinegar

Combine all ingredients in a large Dutch oven; bring to a boil. Cover and cook over medium heat, stirring occasionally, 3 hours or until thickened.

Quickly ladle sauce into hot sterilized jars, leaving ¼-inch headspace. Cover with metal lids, and screw bands tight. Process in boiling-water bath 20 minutes. Serve on vegetables, meat loaf, or omelets. Yield: 4 pints.

BARBECUE SAUCE

6 pounds (about 12) tomatoes, peeled and cored
2 medium onions, quartered
2 cups chopped celery
1½ cups chopped green pepper
2 hot red peppers
1 teaspoon whole peppercorns
1 cup firmly packed brown sugar
1 cup vinegar
2 cloves garlic, minced
1 tablespoon salt
1 tablespoon dry mustard
1 tablespoon paprika
⅛ teaspoon red pepper
1 teaspoon hot sauce

Combine tomatoes, onion, celery, green pepper, and red peppers in a large stockpot; cook over medium heat, stirring occasionally, 30 minutes or until vegetables are tender. Press mixture through a sieve or food mill; return strained mixture to stockpot. Cook over medium heat, stirring occasionally, 30 minutes or until volume is reduced by half.

Tie peppercorns in cheesecloth; add to tomato mixture. Stir in remaining ingredients. Cook, uncovered, over low heat 1½ hours, stirring occasionally. Remove and discard cheesecloth spice bag.

Ladle sauce into hot sterilized jars, leaving ¼-inch headspace. Cover with metal lids, and screw bands tight. Process in boiling-water bath 20 minutes. Use as a basting sauce when roasting beef, pork, or chicken. Yield: about 2½ pints.

Trade card of 1891 illustrates difference between having and not having catsup.

Staples and Charles

APRICOT MUSTARD

1 (10-ounce) package dried
  apricots
2 cups water
¼ cup plus 2 tablespoons
  honey
⅓ cup cream sherry
¼ cup dry mustard
1 tablespoon plus 1½
  teaspoons ground ginger
1 tablespoon curry powder
2 teaspoons almond extract

Place apricots and water in a small saucepan; cover with water. Cover and let stand 1 hour. Cook over medium heat 10 minutes or until soft.

Place half of apricot mixture in container of an electric blender; process until smooth. Repeat procedure with remaining apricot mixture.

Combine pureed apricots with remaining ingredients in a large bowl, mixing well.

Pour mustard into hot sterilized jars. Cover with metal lids, and screw bands tight. Refrigerate 24 hours before serving. Serve with cold meats. Yield: 4 half pints.

R.T. French Company

Mustard packing at the R. T. French Company, c.1915.

DILL MUSTARD

1 cup dry mustard
1 cup vinegar
¾ cup sugar
¼ cup water
1½ teaspoons dried dill
  weed
2 teaspoons salt
2 eggs, lightly beaten

Combine all ingredients, except eggs, in top of a double boiler; cover and let stand at room temperature 4 to 6 hours.

Add beaten egg to reserved mixture, stirring well with a wire whisk. Cook over simmering water, stirring constantly, 8 minutes or until thickened.

Quickly ladle mustard into hot sterilized jars. Cover with metal lids, and screw bands tight. Refrigerate 24 hours before serving. Mustard may be stored in refrigerator up to 3 months. Yield: about 2 half pints.

BEER MUSTARD

1⅓ cups beer
1 cup dry mustard
¼ cup water
2 tablespoons sugar
1 tablespoon plus 1 teaspoon
  white wine vinegar
½ teaspoon ground ginger
½ teaspoon turmeric
1 tablespoon salt
2 eggs, lightly beaten

Combine all ingredients, except eggs, in top of a double boiler; cover and let stand at room temperature 2 to 3 hours.

Add beaten egg to reserved mixture, stirring well with a wire whisk. Cook over simmering water, stirring constantly, 10 minutes or until thickened.

Quickly ladle mustard into hot sterilized jars. Cover with metal lids, and screw bands tight. Refrigerate 24 hours before serving. Mustard may be stored in refrigerator up to 3 months. Serve with meats. Yield: 2 half pints.

HORSERADISH MUSTARD

1 cup dry mustard
¾ cup white wine vinegar
⅓ cup water
¼ cup sugar
3 tablespoons brown sugar
2 teaspoons onion salt
¾ teaspoon caraway seeds
⅛ teaspoon red pepper
2 eggs, lightly beaten
1 tablespoon plus 1½
  teaspoons prepared
  horseradish

Combine first 8 ingredients in top of a double boiler. Cover and let stand 4 to 6 hours.

Add beaten egg to reserved mixture, stirring well. Cook over simmering water, stirring constantly, 8 minutes or until thickened. Stir in horseradish.

Quickly ladle mustard into hot sterilized jars. Cover with metal lids, and screw bands tight. Refrigerate at least 24 hours before serving. Serve with meats. Yield: 2½ half pints.

Exciting gift idea: A nippy mustard sampler.

CHICAGO HOT

2 quarts finely chopped,
  peeled tomatoes
½ cup chopped onion
½ cup chopped celery
1 medium-size sweet red
  pepper, seeded and chopped
2 hot red peppers, chopped
¼ cup grated fresh
  horseradish
½ cup plus 2 tablespoons
  sugar
2 tablespoons mustard seeds
2 tablespoons salt
1 teaspoon red pepper
1 cup vinegar

Combine all ingredients in a
large mixing bowl, stirring well.
  Ladle relish into sterilized
jars. Cover with metal lids, and
screw bands tight. Store in refrigerator until ready to use.
Yield: 11 half pints.

SAUERKRAUT RELISH

2 cups sugar
2 cups chopped celery
1 cup chopped green
  pepper
1 cup chopped onion
1 cup vinegar
1 (16-ounce) can sauerkraut,
  drained
1 (4-ounce) jar pimientos,
  drained and chopped

Combine all ingredients in a
large bowl; stir well. Cover and
refrigerate overnight. Serve immediately with vegetable dishes,
or store in an airtight container
in refrigerator up to 2 weeks.
Yield: 1½ quarts.

*Refrigerators made
by White Mountain,
according to 1890s ad,
were easy to clean.*

PREPARED HORSERADISH

⅔ cup vinegar
¼ cup sugar
1 teaspoon salt
1 teaspoon olive oil
1 cup grated fresh
  horseradish

Combine vinegar, sugar, salt,
and olive oil in a small saucepan, stirring well; cook over low
heat until slightly heated. Place
horseradish in a small mixing
bowl; pour warm mixture over
horseradish, stirring well.
  Ladle horseradish into hot
sterilized jars, leaving ¼-inch
headspace. Cover with metal
lids, and screw bands tight. Process in boiling-water bath 20
minutes. Use as an accompaniment to cold meats. Store in refrigerator until ready to serve.
Yield: about 2 half pints.

PICKLED JALAPEÑO PEPPERS

1 pound jalapeño peppers,
  washed and stems removed
1 cup vinegar
1 cup water
¼ cup olive oil
1 teaspoon salt
1 teaspoon pickling spices

Pack peppers tightly into hot
sterilized jars. Combine remaining ingredients in a non-aluminum saucepan, and bring to a
boil. Remove from heat, and
pour over peppers, leaving ½-
inch headspace. Cover with
metal lids, and screw bands
tight. Store in refrigerator until
ready to use. Yield: 3 half pints.

*Work was painstaking
and cumbersome at the
Heinz plant, 1900, but
uniforms were neat.*

Collection of Kit Barry, Brattleboro, Vermont

CONFECTIONS AND CONFITS

The ability to taste sweetness is born in us, along with the mechanisms for tasting bitter, sour, and salt. Honey was the most concentrated sweet known to the ancients, but in what is now called the Middle East, the only time they had enough of it was in their dreams. Often a household could afford only enough to make the necessary gifts and sacrifices. Figs and dates, on the other hand, were plentiful enough to be eaten fresh and dried. Gift idea: modern backpackers and campers now use dried fruit just as the caravans once did, sometimes mixed with honey and nuts and grain. Certainly Christmas would not be Christmas without a fetching see-through wrapped plate of dates, figs, and nuts. Old Southern recipes for drying figs include storage instructions: put bay leaves between layers to keep out insects. Sure enough, insects avoid bay leaves. Fruit leathers, an extension of the dried fruit idea, are healthful treats we can give our children with good conscience. Vary the fruit: apples, pears, or strawberries.

Refined sugar came so late in the evolution of our food that, like a child of one's old age, it is doted upon sometimes too much. The English had first crack at it — their West Indies colonies grew the cane. To this day, the English consume more sugar per capita than any other nation. Rum is another legacy from the English. Sugar and rum, sugar and brandy (mostly made of native fruits, some imported) were the basis for some of the South's best-kept fruits. This chapter tells how to do them.

Admittedly, we have learned to use some sugar on our own, and nowhere to better advantage than in treating our native pecans, which is lily gilding of the highest order. Advisory: make lots of each recipe because it always happens at the last minute, the realization that "I forgot So-and-So."

Some of us who make fruitcakes like to candy the fruit ourselves. We're the kind who can lose ourselves for a whole day candying flower petals. Some people draw the line at that point, forgivably. Much of holiday baking calls for crystallized citrus rind, but when it is carefully cooked, dried, and given a sugary surface, it makes a gorgeous gift on its own. Rather old-fashioned, to be sure, but it has a wonderful sweetness with a nip to it.

Specialty sweets make ideal gifts for special people. Clockwise from cupcakes with Candied Pansies and Mint Leaves: Almond Acorns, Apricot and Peach leathers.

FLAVORFUL FRUITS AND SWEET SAUCES

APRICOT BALLS

1 (6-ounce) package dried
  apricots
1 (3-ounce) can coconut
⅔ cup chopped pecans
¼ cup sifted powdered sugar
2 teaspoons orange juice
½ cup sugar

Grind together apricots, coconut, and pecans in a large mixing bowl, using coarse blade of a meat grinder. Add powdered sugar and orange juice; stir. Shape into 1-inch balls; roll in sugar. Yield: 3 dozen.

DATE-NUT ROLL

3½ cups sugar
1 cup milk
¼ cup butter or margarine
1 (16-ounce) package pitted
  dates
1 cup chopped pecans
1 teaspoon vanilla extract
Powdered sugar

Combine sugar, milk, and butter in a medium saucepan. Slowly bring to a boil, stirring until sugar dissolves. Stir in dates and pecans. Cover and cook over medium heat 2 to 3 minutes to wash down sugar crystals from sides of pan. Uncover and continue to cook, without stirring, until mixture reaches soft ball stage (240°). Cool to lukewarm (110°). Add vanilla. Beat at medium speed of an electric mixer until mixture is thickened and cool.

Sift powdered sugar on a linen towel. Spoon date mixture onto towel. Divide into 2 portions; shape each portion into 2 rolls, 1½ inches in diameter. Wrap rolls in towel; let stand until set. Remove towel, and cut each roll into ½-inch-thick slices. Yield: 4½ dozen.

Apricot or Date-Nut rolls may be presented whole, then sliced for eating.

APRICOT CANDY ROLL

1 (6-ounce) package dried
  apricots, chopped
3 cups sugar
1 cup half-and-half
½ teaspoon salt
½ cup chopped walnuts
1 teaspoon vanilla extract
Sifted powdered sugar

Combine chopped apricots, 3 cups sugar, half-and-half, and salt in a medium saucepan. Cook over medium heat, stirring until sugar dissolves. Cover and continue to cook over medium heat 2 to 3 minutes to wash down sugar crystals from sides of pan. Uncover and cook, without stirring, until mixture reaches soft ball stage (236°). Remove from heat; let cool to lukewarm (110°). Add walnuts and vanilla. Beat with a wooden spoon until mixture stiffens.

Turn mixture out onto a lightly buttered smooth surface; knead until mixture is smooth and opaque. Divide candy into 3 portions; shape each portion into 6-inch rolls. Dust each roll with powdered sugar. Wrap rolls individually in waxed paper; chill overnight. Cut into ¼-inch-thick slices to serve. Yield: 6 dozen.

Drying Fruit *by Texas folk artist DeCinter Farley.*

HOLIDAY STUFFED FIGS

36 large fresh figs
1½ cups brandy
36 walnut halves
About ¼ cup raisins
Sugar

Soak figs overnight in brandy. Drain; discard brandy. Make a small hole at the round end of each fig, using a small knife.

Break each walnut half into 2 pieces. Insert 2 pieces walnut and 2 raisins into each fig to seal hole.

Roll each stuffed fig in sugar, and place upright on a wire rack. Allow figs to stand, uncovered, overnight to dry completely. Yield: 3 dozen.

FRUIT SWEETS

1 cup dried figs
1 cup raisins
1 cup pitted dates
1 cup chopped pecans or walnuts
Dash of salt
2 tablespoons orange juice
1 teaspoon lemon juice
Sifted powdered sugar
Pecan or walnut halves

Process figs, raisins, dates, and pecans through a food grinder, using coarse blade. Add salt, orange juice, and lemon juice; mix well. Shape mixture into 1-inch balls. Roll balls in powdered sugar. Press a pecan half on top of each ball. Yield: about 4 dozen.

For a holiday delicacy, Southerners must have lots of sweet figs, dried or stuffed, on their party tables. The Greeks and Romans, with a climate similar to ours "down" South, never sat down to a feast without them. Drying figs in the 1800s involved scalding, cooking in syrup, and drying in the sun. They were stored in layers with bay leaves in between to keep insects away. Rank figs high for gift giving this year.

Times were lean in the South in the 1930s, when this family turned their hands to drying apples for the winter food supply.

DRIED APPLE TREATS

½ cup honey
⅓ cup whole wheat flour
¼ cup instant nonfat dry milk
¼ cup butter or margarine
2 tablespoons creamy peanut butter
1 teaspoon vanilla extract
¼ teaspoon salt
1 cup chopped pecans
1 cup sunflower seeds
⅔ cup raisins
⅔ cup chopped dried apples
⅔ cup chopped dried apricots
⅔ cup flaked coconut

Combine honey, flour, milk, and butter in a small saucepan. Bring to a boil; stir well. Remove from heat.

Add peanut butter, vanilla, and salt; mix well. Add remaining ingredients; mix well. Shape into 1-inch balls. Cover and chill. Yield: 4 dozen.

APRICOT LEATHER

1 (6-ounce) package dried apricots
2 cups water
½ cup sugar

Combine apricots and water in a medium saucepan; cover and let soak overnight.

Bring apricot mixture to a boil. Reduce heat; simmer 5 minutes, stirring occasionally. Remove from heat; drain thoroughly, discarding liquid.

Place apricots in container of an electric blender; process until smooth. Return pureed apricots to saucepan; stir in sugar. Bring to a boil; boil 2 minutes, stirring constantly. Remove from heat; let cool 15 minutes.

Line a 15- x 10- x 1-inch jellyroll pan with plastic wrap. Spread apricot mixture evenly in pan. Bake at 150°, with oven door opened slightly, 8 hours or overnight. Cool completely.

Cut apricot leather into 1- x 3-inch strips; roll up each strip. Store in airtight containers. Yield: about 4 dozen.

PEACH LEATHER

6 cups chopped, peeled peaches
½ cup water
1 cup firmly packed light brown sugar
½ cup sugar

Combine peaches and water in a small Dutch oven; cover and simmer 20 minutes or until tender. Remove from heat; drain, discarding liquid. Process peaches in a food mill. Add brown sugar, mix well.

Pour mixture into an ungreased 15- x 10- x 1-inch jellyroll pan. Bake at 300° for 2½ hours, stirring mixture every 30 minutes.

Line a 15- x 10- x 1-inch jellyroll pan with plastic wrap. Spread mixture evenly in pan. Bake at 150°, with oven door opened slightly, 8 hours or overnight. Let cool; cut into 5-inch squares. Sprinkle both sides of squares evenly with ½ cup sugar; roll up each square. Wrap individually in plastic wrap. Store in refrigerator. Yield: ½ dozen.

BRANDIED FRUIT

B randy, a shortened version of brandywine (Dutch for burnt wine), has a long and honorable history. It is distilled from wine, preferably white wine, or from marc, the residue left in the wine press. Cognac, most prime of the French brandies, comes only from the district of Cognac and is so labeled. All others are merely brandy. Brandies are also made of peaches or plums, as in the potent Balkan slivovitz. When we use brandy as an ingredient, especially in foods for gift giving or festive times, we should think quality.

BRANDIED NECTARINES

1½ cups sugar
1½ cups firmly packed brown sugar
2 cups water
3 pounds nectarines (about 12), peeled and halved
¾ cup brandy

Combine sugar and water in a large heavy skillet. Cook over medium heat, stirring constantly, until mixture comes to a boil and sugar dissolves. Add nectarines. Cover and reduce heat; simmer 4 minutes. Turn fruit; cover and continue to simmer 4 minutes or just until tender.

Pour ¼ cup brandy into each hot sterilized jar. Pack nectarines into jars, reserving syrup.

Cook reserved syrup over medium heat 15 minutes or until slightly thickened. Pour over nectarines, leaving ½-inch headspace. Cover with metal lids, and screw bands only fingertip tight. Process in boiling-water bath 10 minutes. Let stand in a warm, dark place 1 month before serving. Yield: 3 pints.

1 (16-ounce) can sliced peaches in light syrup, drained
1 (17-ounce) can apricot halves, drained
1 (20-ounce) can pineapple chunks, undrained
1 (8-ounce) jar maraschino cherries, undrained
5 cups sugar
1⅔ cups brandy

Combine all ingredients in a large glass mixing bowl; stir gently. Ladle mixture into clean jars; cover with metal lids, and screw bands only fingertip tight. Let stand in a warm, dark place 3 weeks, stirring fruit every other day with a wooden spoon.

Serve fruit over ice cream, orange sherbet, or pound cake, reserving at least 1½ cups fruit mixture to use as a starter at all times. Yield: 2½ quarts.

Note: To replenish starter, add 1 cup sugar and one of the first 3 ingredients every 1 to 3 weeks, alternating fruit each time; stir gently. Cover and let stand at room temperature 3 days before serving.

Nectarines, 1839 color plate.

TUTTI-FRUTTI

The audacious flavor blend of fruits fermented in alcohol is old, although just how old is open to question. Southerners sometimes call it Civil War sauce, but it is difficult to pin down. At Christmastime, though, the various mixtures surface under this name or that. It may be Dried Fruit in Rum, which gets made once, but is used in several ways: with ice cream or cake, of course, but equally nice used as a relish-garnish with roasted meats. Then there are the holiday desserts of vanilla ice cream served with syrupy spoonfuls of Tutti-Frutti or Brandied Fruit, which are meant to be replenished.

Ingredients needed over a 5-week period:

1 (750 ml) bottle brandy
11 cups sugar, divided
2 quarts fresh stawberries, washed, hulled, and divided
4 cups fresh pineapple cubes
2 cups sliced, peeled fresh peaches
1 (9-ounce) package raisins

Week 1: Combine brandy and 1 cup sugar in a 3-gallon crock; stir well. Stir in 1 quart strawberries. Cover and let stand at room temperature 1 week.

Week 2: Stir in remaining strawberries and 4 cups sugar. Cover and let stand at room temperature 1 week.

Week 3: Stir in fresh pineapple and 4 cups sugar. Cover and let stand at room temperature 1 week.

Week 4: Stir in peaches and 2 cups sugar. Cover and let stand at room temperature 1 week.

Week 5: Stir in raisins. Cover and let stand at room temperature 1 week. Serve over ice cream or pound cake. Yield: 5 quarts.

DRIED FRUIT IN RUM

10 dried whole peaches
3 (15-ounce) packages golden raisins
20 dried whole prunes
14 dried whole figs
20 dried whole apricots
About 1 quart light rum

Arrange peaches around the bottom inner sides of clean rubber-seal jars. Fill jars with enough raisins to press peaches firmly against sides. Repeat procedure, alternating prunes, figs, and apricots in place of peaches, until jars are filled with fruit.

Pour rum over fruit in each jar, leaving ½-inch headspace. Place rubber seal on rim of each jar. Secure glass lids firmly over seals by clamping metal clasps. Store at room temperature 3 weeks. Yield: 2 quarts.

Brandied Fruit and Tutti-Frutti (front); elegance in a jar that can be replenished.

84

BUTTERSCOTCH SAUCE

⅔ cup firmly packed brown
  sugar
⅓ cup light corn syrup
¼ cup plus 1 tablespoon
  butter or margarine, melted
¼ cup water
1 egg yolk, well beaten
½ cup chopped pecans,
  toasted

Combine all ingredients, except pecans, in top of a double
boiler; stir well. Cook over boiling water, stirring frequently,
until mixture thickens and is
smooth. Stir in toasted pecans.

Pour sauce into hot sterilized
jars. Cover with lids, and screw
bands tight. Serve warm over
ice cream or pound cake. Store
jars in refrigerator. Yield: 2 half
pints.

CARAMEL SAUCE

1 cup firmly packed light
  brown sugar
½ cup sugar
½ cup light corn syrup
½ cup half-and-half
¼ cup butter or margarine
1 cup cashews

Combine sugar and syrup in a
medium-size heavy saucepan;
stir well. Cook over medium
heat, stirring constantly, until
sugar dissolves. Cover and continue to cook over medium heat
2 to 3 minutes to wash down
sugar crystals from sides of pan.
Uncover and cook, without stirring, until mixture reaches soft
ball stage (234°). Remove from
heat; stir in half-and-half and
butter. Add cashews, stirring
well. Serve warm over ice cream
or plain cake. Store in an airtight container in refrigerator.
Yield: 2½ cups.

*In 1939, a San Antonio
newspaper featured this
lady in a series on
engaged women preparing
for their role as housewives.*

CHOCOLATE SAUCE

½ cup butter or margarine
4 (1-ounce) squares
  unsweetened chocolate
3 cups sugar
¼ teaspoon salt
1 (12-ounce) can evaporated
  milk
1 teaspoon vanilla extract

Melt butter and chocolate in top of a double boiler over simmering water. Remove from heat; stir in sugar and salt. Gradually add milk, stirring well to blend. Cook over simmering water 7 minutes, stirring constantly. Remove from heat; stir in vanilla. Cool slightly; serve over ice cream or pound cake. Store in refrigerator. Yield: 1 quart.

RAISIN-CHOCOLATE SAUCE

1¼ cups sugar
¼ cup plus 2 tablespoons
  cocoa
3 tablespoons butter or
  margarine
2 cups plus 1 tablespoon
  water, divided
2 teaspoons cornstarch
½ teaspoon vanilla extract
Dash of salt
1 cup raisins

Combine sugar, cocoa, butter, and 2 cups water in a small saucepan; bring to a boil. Boil 5 minutes, stirring until sugar dissolves. Dissolve cornstarch in 1 tablespoon water; add to cocoa mixture, stirring well. Return to a boil. Reduce heat; simmer, stirring until mixture thickens. Remove from heat; stir in vanilla, salt, and raisins. Serve warm or chilled over ice cream or cake. Store in refrigerator. Yield: 2½ cups.

HOT FUDGE SAUCE

2 (1-ounce) squares
  semisweet chocolate
½ cup butter or margarine
1½ cups sugar
1 cup evaporated milk
1 teaspoon vanilla extract

Melt chocolate and butter in top of a double boiler over boiling water. Add sugar and milk; mix until well blended. Cook over simmering water, stirring occasionally, 2 hours or until sauce thickens and is smooth. Stir in vanilla. Serve warm over ice cream, pound cake, or fruit. Store in covered jars in refrigerator. Yield: 2 cups.

MARY RANDOLPH'S LEMON CREAM SAUCE

¾ cup butter or margarine
2 cups sugar
Grated rind and juice of 4
  lemons
4 eggs, well beaten

Melt butter in top of a double boiler over boiling water. Gradually stir in sugar and lemon rind and juice. Gradually stir 1 tablespoon hot mixture into beaten egg; add to remaining hot mixture, stirring constantly. Cook over medium heat, stirring until sauce thickens.

Pour lemon sauce into hot sterilized jars. Cover with metal lids, and screw bands tight. Serve warm or chilled over ice cream, pound cake, or steamed pudding. Store in refrigerator until ready to serve. Yield: about 4 half pints.

Chocolate (left) stands tall among dessert sauces. Sherry (left rear), Caramel, and Lemon Cream sauces complete picture.

Opening this can required study, c.1890.

Collection of Kit Barry, Brattleboro, Vermont

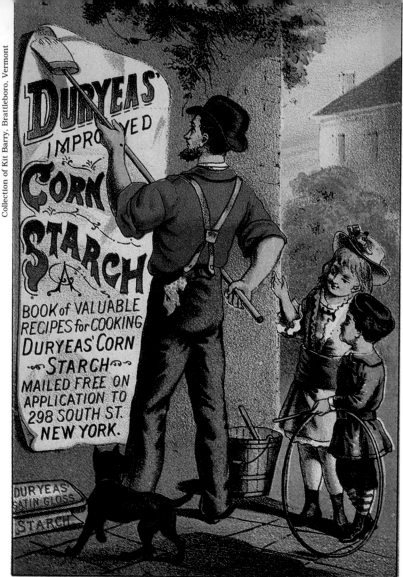

Foldover ad of another ad getting posted, c.1885.

RUM BUTTER SAUCE

1 cup butter, softened
2 cups sifted powdered sugar
2 eggs, well beaten
¼ cup dark rum

Cream butter in top of a double boiler. Add sugar; beat well. Add eggs and rum; beat well. Cook over boiling water, stirring until mixture thickens.

Spoon sauce into hot sterilized jars. Cover with metal lids; screw bands tight. Serve sauce warm over bread pudding or fresh fruit. Store in refrigerator. Yield: 2 half pints.

SHERRY SAUCE

4 egg yolks, well beaten
1 cup sugar
1 teaspoon all-purpose flour
1 cup sherry
1 cup whipping cream

Combine egg yolks, sugar, flour, and sherry in top of a double boiler; stir well. Cook over boiling water, stirring until thickened. Chill. Stir in whipping cream.

Pour sauce into hot sterilized jars. Cover with metal lids; screw bands tight. Serve chilled over fruitcakes or steamed puddings. Store in refrigerator. Yield: about 3 half pints.

FIG SAUCE

12 to 15 fresh ripe figs, peeled and chopped
½ cup sugar
1 cup water
1 tablespoon butter or margarine
1 tablespoon cornstarch
3 tablespoons lemon juice

Combine figs, sugar, water, and butter in a saucepan; bring to a boil. Reduce heat; simmer 5 to 8 minutes or until tender.

Combine cornstarch and lemon juice, mixing until smooth. Stir into fig mixture; cook over low heat, stirring constantly, until thickened and bubbly. Serve sauce warm over ice cream. Yield: 3½ cups.

ORANGE SAUCE

1 cup sugar
3 tablespoons cornstarch
½ teaspoon salt
1 cup water
2 tablespoons butter or margarine
2 teaspoons grated orange rind
¾ cup fresh orange juice

Combine sugar, cornstarch, salt, and water in a medium saucepan. Stir until dry ingredients dissolve. Cook over low heat, stirring constantly, 5 minutes or until mixture is clear. Add butter, orange rind and juice; stir well. Continue to cook, stirring constantly, 5 minutes or until sauce thickens.

Spoon sauce into hot sterilized jars. Cover with metal lids, and screw bands tight. Serve warm over steamed puddings or plain cakes. Store in refrigerator. Yield: 3 half pints.

CANDIED FRUITS, NUTS, AND FLOWERS

CANDIED CITRUS PEEL

½ cup lemon-peel strips
   (¼-inch wide)
½ cup lime-peel strips
   (¼-inch wide)
½ cup orange-peel strips
   (¼-inch wide)
½ cup grapefruit-peel strips
   (¼-inch wide)
1 cup sugar
½ cup water
Additional sugar

Combine citrus peel and cold water to cover in a small saucepan; slowly bring to a boil. Reduce heat; simmer 10 minutes, stirring occasionally. Drain.

Repeat boiling and draining procedure 3 times.

Combine 1 cup sugar and water in a small saucepan; bring mixture to a boil. Add peel. Reduce heat; simmer, stirring frequently, 20 minutes or until liquid is almost absorbed and peel becomes translucent. Drain well.

Roll peel, a few pieces at a time, in additional sugar. Arrange in a single layer on a wire rack; let dry 8 hours. Store in an airtight container. Yield: about 1½ cups.

Note: Citrus Peel may be used in baking or stored in airtight tins as a confection.

CHOCOLATE-COVERED CITRUS PEEL

8 ounces chocolate,
   processed for dipping
Candied Citrus Peel

Place chocolate in a medium-size stoneware bowl; set bowl in a pan of boiling water. Stir constantly with a wooden spoon just until chocolate melts (too much heat will affect dipping quality of chocolate).

Dip each piece of Candied Citrus Peel in chocolate, using a dipping fork; remove to waxed paper to set. Store in an airtight container in refrigerator. Yield: about 1½ cups.

Grapefruits, oranges, and a smile say "sunshine" from Florida, c.1940.

A FLORIDA BLOSSOM AMONG GRAPEFRUIT AND ORANGES

Candied Pineapple and Cherries; Fruit Glacé.

FRUIT GLACÉ

1 cup sugar
1 cup light corn syrup
⅓ cup water
1 pint strawberries, washed
with hulls intact
2 oranges, peeled, sectioned,
and seeded

Combine sugar, syrup, and water in a small saucepan. Cook over medium heat, stirring constantly, until sugar dissolves. Cover and continue to cook over medium heat 2 to 3 minutes to wash down sugar crystals from sides of pan. Uncover and cook, without stirring, until mixture reaches soft crack stage (280°).

Remove from heat, and place pan over hot water. Working rapidly, dip fruit into hot syrup, using a fork. Place fruit on a buttered baking sheet to harden. Let cool. Serve within 2 hours. Yield: 1 pint strawberries and 2 oranges.

Crystallized fruit peel is a Southern Christmas tradition. How to: Working with the equivalent of 8 large oranges or lemons, and/or small grapefruit, take off peel; cut into narrow strips. (Juiced halves may be scraped out after the first boiling and cut with scissors.) Starting with cold water, bring peel to a full boil; drain. Repeat. Cover with cold water again, and simmer until tender; drain. Combine 3½ cups each of sugar and water in a 4-quart saucepan. Stir until mixture comes to a boil. Add rind. Reduce heat, and cook, shaking pan to prevent scorching, until fruit is clear and almost all liquid is absorbed. Drain on racks. Roll in coarse sugar; dry on racks overnight. For an elegant gift, pack in silver boxes.

CANDIED PINEAPPLE AND CHERRIES

2 (20-ounce) cans sliced
pineapple, undrained
2 cups sugar
½ cup light corn syrup
3 (8-ounce) jars maraschino
cherries, drained

Drain pineapple, reserving 1⅔ cups pineapple juice.

Combine pineapple juice, sugar, and syrup in a large Dutch oven. Bring to a boil, stirring constantly. Cook over medium heat, without stirring, until mixture reaches soft ball stage (234°). Add reserved pineapple slices; return syrup mixture to a boil. Reduce heat; simmer 20 minutes or until pineapple is translucent. Carefully remove pineapple with a fork, and drain on wire racks.

Add cherries to syrup, and return to a boil. Reduce heat; simmer 20 minutes, stirring occasionally. Remove cherries, and drain on wire racks. Let fruit dry on racks 24 hours. Store in airtight containers, or freeze. Yield: 20 pineapple slices and about 10 dozen cherries.

SALTED ALMONDS

2 pounds blanched whole
almonds
1 tablespoon butter or
margarine, melted
1 tablespoon salt

Combine all ingredients in a
large cast-iron skillet; stir well.
Cook over medium heat, stirring constantly, until almonds
are lightly browned. Let cool,
and store in an airtight container. Yield: about 3½ cups.

CANDIED ALMONDS

2 cups blanched whole
almonds
1 cup sugar
3 tablespoons water

Place almonds in a shallow
baking pan. Bake at 250° for 15
minutes or until lightly toasted.
Remove from oven, and set
aside.

Combine sugar and water in a
medium saucepan. Cook over
medium heat, stirring occasionally, until mixture reaches soft
ball stage (240°).

Remove from heat, and place
pan over hot water to keep
warm. Working rapidly, dip almonds, a few at a time, into hot
syrup. Remove, one at a time,
using a fork or candy dipper.
Place on waxed paper to harden.
Let cool completely. Remove
from waxed paper, and store in
an airtight container. Yield:
about 3 cups.

ALMOND ACORNS

1 pound blanched whole
almonds, toasted
1 (6-ounce) package
semisweet chocolate
morsels, melted
3 (1.75-ounce) jars chocolate
sprinkles

Dip the wide end of each almond halfway into melted chocolate. Dip the chocolate end of
each almond into chocolate
sprinkles. Place on waxed
paper; let chocolate harden. Remove from waxed paper; store in
an airtight container. (Do not
layer.) Yield: about 2 cups.

Sun drying almonds in special bins, c.1915.

Marzipan: A good way to display artistic talent.

CITRUS-CANDIED PECANS

2 cups sugar
1 tablespoon all-purpose flour
½ cup plus 2 tablespoons milk
1 tablespoon butter
Grated rind and juice of 1 orange
Juice of ½ lemon
4 cups pecan halves

Combine sugar and flour in a medium-size heavy saucepan; mix well. Add milk and butter; bring to a boil, stirring constantly. Stir in orange rind and juice and lemon juice. Cook over medium heat, stirring occasionally, until mixture reaches soft ball stage (240°).

Remove from heat; stir in pecans. Beat with a wooden spoon until mixture begins to thicken. Working rapidly, spread mixture on waxed paper; separate pecans with a fork. Let cool. Store in airtight containers. Yield: about 6 cups.

MARZIPAN

1 (8-ounce) can almond paste
¼ cup butter, softened
2 tablespoons light corn syrup
2 tablespoons kirsch or other cherry-flavored brandy
¼ teaspoon almond extract
2¼ cups sifted powdered sugar
Liquid food coloring

Combine almond paste and butter in a medium mixing bowl; beat until creamy. Add syrup, kirsch, and almond extract, beating well. Turn mixture out onto a board or marble slab dusted with powdered sugar; gradually knead 2¼ cups sifted powdered sugar into dough.

Knead desired food coloring into dough; mold into small fruit shapes. Let dry overnight on waxed paper. Store in refrigerator in an airtight container. Yield: 2¼ cups.

COFFEE PECANS

2 cups toasted pecan halves
¼ cup sugar
2 teaspoons instant coffee granules
¼ teaspoon ground allspice
⅛ teaspoon salt
2 tablespoons water

Combine all ingredients in a medium saucepan; mix well. Bring to a boil. Cook over medium heat 3 minutes, stirring constantly. Spread pecans on waxed paper, and separate with a fork. Cool. Yield: 2 cups.

MINTED PECANS

1 cup sugar
1 cup water
1 tablespoon light corn syrup
⅛ teaspoon salt
6 large marshmallows
½ teaspoon peppermint oil
3 cups chopped pecans

Combine sugar, water, syrup, and salt in a small Dutch oven. Cook over medium heat, stirring constantly, until sugar dissolves. Cover and continue to cook over medium heat 2 to 3 minutes to wash down sugar crystals from sides of pan. Uncover and cook, without stirring, until mixture reaches thread stage (230°). Remove from heat, and add marshmallows. Stir until marshmallows melt. Add peppermint oil and pecans, stirring well.

Working rapidly, drop pecan mixture by teaspoonfuls onto waxed paper. Let cool; store in airtight containers. Yield: about 5 cups.

ORANGE-CANDIED PECANS

3 cups firmly packed brown sugar
1 cup orange juice
1½ tablespoons butter or margarine
1 teaspoon grated orange rind
1 pound pecan or walnut halves

Combine sugar and orange juice in a large non-aluminum saucepan; stir well. Cook over medium heat, stirring occasionally, until mixture reaches soft ball stage (240°).

Remove from heat; stir in butter and orange rind. Beat at high speed of an electric mixer 8 minutes or until mixture thickens and begins to cool. Stir in pecans.

Spread mixture in a buttered 15- x 10- x 1-inch jellyroll pan. Separate pecans, using 2 forks. Let cool completely. Store in airtight containers. Yield: 8 cups.

FROSTED PECANS

1 cup sugar
1 teaspoon ground cinnamon
1 teaspoon salt
1 egg white
1 tablespoon water
2 cups pecan halves

Combine sugar, cinnamon, and salt in a small mixing bowl; set aside.

Combine egg white (at room temperature) and water in a medium mixing bowl; beat until stiff peaks form. Add pecans; stir to coat well. Remove pecans, one at a time; roll each in reserved sugar mixture.

Place pecans on a lightly greased 15- x 10- x 1-inch jellyroll pan. Bake at 275° for 1 hour. Cool slightly in pan. Remove to wire racks to cool completely. Store in an airtight container. Yield: about 4 cups.

Pecans with a pedigree on exhibit at Tri-State Fair in Memphis, c.1935.

The pecan has given the Southern cook a corner on the sweetmeat market. Just cast a glance over the party table; there will be pecans in the candy dish even if you've already had some, salted and toasted, with cocktails. To nut "factories" such as those in Texas and Oklahoma, pecans are money in the bank. Over four hundred years have passed since Cabeza de Vaca, the Spanish explorer, was captured by the Indians in what is now Texas and found it their custom to repair to the riverbanks and stay alive all winter by eating pecans and very little else. Pecans are a luxury now, but we continue to indulge ourselves and our dear ones at gift-giving time.

PRALINE DROPS

1 egg white
1 tablespoon all-purpose flour
½ teaspoon salt
½ teaspoon almond extract
1 cup firmly packed brown
  sugar
2 cups pecan halves

Combine egg white (at room temperature), flour, salt, and almond extract in a medium mixing bowl; beat until soft peaks form. Gradually add sugar, 1 tablespoon at a time, beating until stiff peaks form. (Do not underbeat mixture.) Fold in pecans.

Drop each pecan half onto a well-greased baking sheet. Bake at 300° for 25 minutes. Turn oven off; cool in oven at least 1 hour. (Do not open oven door.) Remove pecans from baking sheet; store in an airtight container. Yield: about 4 cups.

SUGARED WALNUTS

1 cup firmly packed brown
  sugar
½ cup sugar
½ cup commercial sour
  cream
1 teaspoon vanilla extract
2 (3-ounce) packages walnut
  halves

Combine sugar and sour cream in a Dutch oven; stir well. Bring to a boil; boil, without stirring, until mixture reaches soft ball stage (238°). Stir in vanilla and walnuts.

Quickly turn walnuts out onto a buttered baking sheet; separate with a fork. Let cool; store in an airtight container. Yield: about 2½ cups.

Southern cooking, especially of the sort represented in this book, could not have evolved without sucrose. Before 1747, when it was found that a certain beet contains about 15% sugar, sugarcane was the only source. Grown in prehistoric Asia, sugarcane was cropped in Sicily as early as the eighth century; Arabs brought it to Spain around the eleventh century. But until the late 1700s, it was grown mainly for chewing. New varieties from Java, richer in sucrose, helped give rise to the sugar industry as we know it today.

Inspecting sugarcane in Florida, c.1920.

raline Drops (front); Coffee Walnuts and Holiday Nuts (page 96).

Separating nutmeats from the shells, c.1915.

COFFEE WALNUTS

1 cup firmly packed light
  brown sugar
½ cup sugar
½ cup commercial sour
  cream
1 tablespoon instant coffee
  granules
1 teaspoon vanilla extract
2½ cups walnut halves

Combine sugar, sour cream,
and coffee in a medium saucepan. Cook over medium heat,
stirring constantly, until sugar
dissolves. Cover and continue to
cook over medium heat 2 to 3
minutes to wash down sugar
crystals from sides of pan. Uncover and cook, without stirring, until mixture reaches soft
ball stage (234°).

Remove from heat; stir in vanilla and walnuts, mixing well.
Stir just until mixture begins to
cool. Pour mixture into a buttered 15- x 10- x 1-inch jellyroll
pan. Quickly separate walnuts
with a fork. Let cool, and store
in an airtight container. Yield:
4½ cups.

CINNAMON WALNUTS

1 cup sugar
½ teaspoon ground cinnamon
⅛ teaspoon cream of tartar
¼ cup boiling water
½ teaspoon vanilla extract
1½ cups walnut halves

Combine sugar, cinnamon,
cream of tartar, and water in a
medium-size heavy saucepan;
stir until well blended. Cook
over medium heat, stirring occasionally, until mixture
reaches soft ball stage (240°).

Remove from heat; stir in vanilla and walnuts. Beat with a
wooden spoon until mixture
begins to thicken. Quickly
spread walnuts on waxed paper;
separate with a fork. Let cool.
Store in airtight containers.
Yield: about 3 cups.

HOLIDAY NUTS

4 cups pecan halves
1½ cups blanched whole
  almonds
1¾ cups walnut
  pieces
4 egg whites
Dash of salt
2 cups sugar
1 cup butter, melted

Spread pecans, almonds, and
walnuts evenly in a 15- x 10- x
1-inch jellyroll pan. Bake at 250°
for 20 minutes or until lightly
toasted. Remove from oven; set
aside.

Beat egg whites (at room temperature) and salt in a large
mixing bowl until soft peaks
form. Gradually add sugar, 1 tablespoon at a time, beating until
stiff peaks form. Fold in toasted
pecans, almonds, and walnuts.

Pour melted butter into jellyroll pan. Spread nut mixture
evenly over butter. Bake at 300°
for 50 minutes, stirring every 15
minutes. Let cool completely.
Store in airtight containers.
Yield: 12 cups.

SUGAR AND SPICE NUTS

1 egg white
1 teaspoon water
½ cup sugar
½ teaspoon salt
1½ teaspoons ground
   cinnamon
½ teaspoon ground coriander
½ teaspoon ground nutmeg
1 cup blanched whole
   almonds
1 cup pecan halves
¼ cup butter, melted

Combine egg white (at room temperature) and water; beat until foamy.

Combine sugar, salt, cinnamon, coriander, and nutmeg; stir well. Gradually add to egg white mixture, beating until soft peaks form. Fold in almonds and pecans.

Spread mixture evenly in a 13- x 9- x 2-inch baking pan. Bake at 225° for 1 hour or until nuts are dry; stir mixture every 20 minutes.

Remove nuts to waxed paper, and separate with a fork. Brush with melted butter. Let dry. Store in an airtight container. Yield: 2 cups.

CANDIED PANSIES, MINT LEAVES, AND ROSE PETALS

1 egg white
12 pansies, rinsed and
   drained
12 rose petals, rinsed and
   drained
12 mint leaves (or lemon
   balm leaves), rinsed and
   drained
½ cup sugar

Beat egg white (at room temperature) until foamy. Using a small artist's brush, coat each pansy petal, rose petal, and mint leaf with egg white. Shake to remove any excess egg white. Sprinkle sugar over petals and leaves. Separate petals of pansies. Place on a wire rack. Let stand overnight or until dry. Store in airtight containers. Yield: 3 dozen.

ary MacNicol's *Flower Cookery, The Art of Cooking with Flowers*, 1967, is a rarity among cookbooks, equal parts charm and erudition. Flowers are edible in more ways than we imagine. She gives a recipe for pansy wine "good for addling wits" and quotes Robert Browning: "Pansies, eyes that laugh, bear beauty's prize/From violets, eyes that dream." Sugary, laughing eyes, when placed on a cupcake, will evoke a smile on any occasion.

Everything needed for candying flowers here.

THE CANDY BOX

The confections comprising this chapter necessarily skirt the issue of professional candy making, being rather a homemaker's guide to making candies easily accomplished by the amateur with home utensils and ingredients. A few words about those implements may be in order.

For utensils, heavy-bottomed pans are necessary; the best material for the purpose is probably aluminum that is lined, inside and out, with stainless steel. Pans should be large enough to allow for boiling space at the top and shaped with straight sides. Important factor: candy mixture must be deep enough in the pan to immerse the business end of the thermometer.

In addition to a high quality thermometer, making candy on a regular basis requires a marble slab on which to pour out cooked fondant and brittles or to drop lollipops — or all candies, in fact, in which rapid cooling is necessary. Many cooks have fared well for years without the marble, using pans or platters (at risk of breaking platters with the high heat of brittles, lollipops, etc.) Many candymakers, intent on emulating the professionals, use marble even if they must carry an old tabletop into the kitchen on a designated "candy-making day." But a new, polished tabletop would be marred by the heat.

In amassing enough candy over, say, a month's time, to supply an orgy of Christmas giving, attention must be paid to keeping it safe in storage. Next to the depredations of one's own family, moisture is candy's greatest enemy. Use large tins with tight lids. Pack only one variety in each tin, even if pieces are wrapped separately. Candies will pick up flavors from one another. Black walnuts and peppermint are probably the worst sinners in this respect.

At packing time, with all the creativity at your command, assemble the prettiest containers possible. Glass dishes, coffee tins wrapped in festive paper, . . . Use colorful bonbon cups for small candies, "kiss papers" from the confectioner's supply house or cut waxed paper for wrapping candy bars and squares. To let your joy in giving be totally reflected in the gift you have so carefully prepared, the packaging must be as creative as the food.

Clockwise from center front: Black Walnut Brittle, Georgia Nuggets (in colorful bags), Solger's Truffles, Sour Cream Fudge, Pecan Toffee, Chocolate Fudge, Texas Millionaires, and Seafoam Candy.

DIVINITY, MARSHMALLOWS, AND PASTES

Sampling candy on a winter outing, North Carolina, c.1900.

DIVINITY FUDGE

3 cups sugar
½ cup water
⅓ cup light corn syrup
Dash of salt
2 egg whites
1 cup chopped walnuts
½ cup coarsely chopped
   maraschino cherries
1 teaspoon vanilla extract

Combine sugar, water, syrup, and salt in a 3-quart saucepan; cook over low heat, stirring constantly, until sugar dissolves. Cover and cook over medium heat 2 to 3 minutes to wash down sugar crystals from sides of pan. Uncover and cook over high heat, without stirring, until mixture reaches firm ball stage (242°).

Beat egg whites (at room temperature) in a large mixing bowl until stiff peaks form. Add half of hot syrup in a thin, steady stream, beating constantly at high speed of an electric mixer. Cook remaining hot syrup over medium heat, without stirring, until mixture reaches hard ball stage (260°). Gradually pour in a thin, steady stream over egg white mixture, beating constantly at high speed of an electric mixer. Continue beating 5 to 10 minutes or until mixture holds its shape when dropped from a spoon. Stir in walnuts, cherries, and vanilla.

Drop mixture by teaspoonfuls onto waxed paper; cool completely. Store in airtight containers in a cool place. Yield: about 3 dozen.

If Divinity Fudge begins to set up before the dropping is done, set candy over hot water; stir to keep it workable. Easier than dropping, and attractive: pour candy onto buttered surface, swirl top with spatula, and cut into squares. To make peanut butter pinwheels, omit nuts and cherries. Quickly spread candy to ½-inch thickness; spread with 1 cup warm peanut butter. Cut in half lengthwise; roll from long sides. Wrap in waxed paper; slice when set. Give in an assortment.

COFFEE DIVINITY

2½ cups sugar
½ cup light corn syrup
½ cup water
¼ teaspoon salt
2 egg whites
2 tablespoons instant coffee
  granules
1 teaspoon vanilla extract
1 cup chopped walnuts

Combine sugar, syrup, water, and salt in a small Dutch oven, stirring well; cook over low heat, stirring constantly, until sugar dissolves. Cover and cook over medium heat 2 to 3 minutes to wash down sugar crystals from sides of pan. Uncover and cook, without stirring, until mixture reaches soft ball stage (240°).

Beat egg whites (at room temperature) in a large mixing bowl until stiff peaks form. Gradually add half of hot syrup in a thin, steady stream, beating constantly at high speed of an electric mixer.

Cook remaining hot syrup, without stirring, until mixture reaches firm ball stage (248°). Gradually pour in a thin, steady stream over egg white mixture, beating constantly at high speed of electric mixer. Add coffee and vanilla; continue beating until mixture loses its gloss and holds its shape. Stir in chopped walnuts.

Drop mixture by tablespoonfuls onto waxed paper. Cool completely. Store in airtight containers in a cool place. Yield: about 4 dozen.

SEAFOAM CANDY

4 cups firmly packed brown
  sugar
1 cup water
1 teaspoon vanilla extract
2 egg whites
1 cup chopped pecans

Combine sugar and water in a large Dutch oven; cook over medium heat, stirring constantly, until sugar dissolves. Cover and continue to cook over medium heat 2 to 3 minutes to wash down sugar crystals from sides of pan. Uncover and cook, without stirring, until mixture reaches firm ball stage (242°). Remove from heat, and stir in vanilla.

Beat egg whites (at room temperature) in a large mixing bowl until stiff peaks form; add hot syrup in a thin, steady stream, beating constantly at high speed of an electric mixer until mixture thickens and cools. Quickly fold in chopped pecans, and drop mixture by tablespoonfuls onto buttered waxed paper. Cool at least 1 hour. Store in airtight containers in a cool place. Do not freeze. Yield: about 5 dozen.

Sweets to tempt the angels are carried by the smiling lady on this trade card from the 1890s.

Pure Candies Our Specialty.

HONEY-PISTACHIO NOUGAT

1 cup sugar
½ cup water
3 tablespoons light corn
  syrup
½ cup honey
2 egg whites
2½ cups toasted almonds,
  coarsely chopped
½ cup toasted pistachio nuts,
  coarsely chopped
1 teaspoon vanilla extract
Cornstarch

Combine sugar, water, and syrup in a small Dutch oven, stirring well; cook over medium heat, stirring constantly, until sugar dissolves. Cover and cook 2 to 3 minutes to wash down sugar crystals from sides of pan.

Uncover and cook, without stirring, until mixture reaches soft crack stage (280°).

Cook honey in a small saucepan over medium heat until thoroughly heated. Add honey to syrup mixture, and continue cooking until mixture reaches soft crack stage (290°).

Beat egg whites (at room temperature) in a large ovenproof mixing bowl until stiff peaks form. Add hot syrup in a thin stream, beating constantly at high speed of an electric mixer. Place mixing bowl in boiling water, and continue beating until mixture is stiff and holds its shape. Stir in chopped al-

monds, pistachios, and vanilla.

Press mixture evenly in a buttered 13- x 9- x 2-inch baking pan that has been sprinkled with cornstarch. Cover mixture with buttered waxed paper; place another 13- x 9- x 2-inch baking pan on top of waxed paper. Weigh down top pan with a heavy object. Let stand overnight to set.

Cut candy into 1-inch squares; wrap individually in waxed paper or colored cellophane, if desired. Yield: about 10 dozen.

Note: Honey-Pistachio Nougat squares may be dipped into melted chocolate, if desired.

An old tradition enacted at a Tennessee state park, 1939.

Tennessee State Library and Archives

MARSHMALLOWS

4 cups sugar
1¾ cups water, divided
4 envelopes unflavored
   gelatin
1 tablespoon vanilla extract
½ cup powdered sugar
½ cup cornstarch

Combine 4 cups sugar and 1 cup water in a 3-quart saucepan; stir well. Cover and let stand 30 minutes.

Combine gelatin and remaining water in a large mixing bowl; let stand 30 minutes.

Cook sugar and water over medium heat, stirring until mixture comes to a boil. Wash off sugar crystals from sides of pan, using a brush dipped in cold water. Continue to cook, without stirring, until mixture reaches firm ball stage (244°).

Pour hot syrup in a thin stream over gelatin mixture, beating constantly at high speed of an electric mixer. Continue beating 30 minutes; beat in vanilla.

Sift together powdered sugar and cornstarch in a 15- x 10- x 1-inch jellyroll pan. Spread marshmallow mixture evenly in pan. Let dry at least 12 hours.

Turn candy out onto waxed paper. Cut into 1-inch squares or circles, rolling marshmallows in excess powdered sugar mixture. Store in airtight containers. Yield: about 12½ dozen.

Homemade Marshmallows, round or square: sensational!

CATHEDRAL CANDY

1 cup butterscotch morsels
½ cup graham cracker
   crumbs
2 tablespoons butter or
   margarine, melted
1 egg, lightly beaten
3 cups colored miniature
   marshmallows
½ cup chopped roasted
   peanuts
1 cup flaked coconut

Melt butterscotch morsels in top of a double boiler over simmering water. Remove from heat, and stir in graham cracker crumbs, melted butter, and beaten egg. Cool slightly.

Add marshmallows and peanuts to butterscotch mixture, stirring well. Shape dough into a roll, 2 inches in diameter; wrap in waxed paper, and chill thoroughly.

Unwrap roll, and press coconut evenly over surface of roll. Cut into ¼-inch-thick slices. Yield: about 4 dozen.

TURKISH DELIGHT

5 envelopes unflavored
  gelatin
⅔ cup orange juice
2 cups sugar
½ cup water
1½ teaspoons lemon extract
½ cup powdered sugar
¼ cup cornstarch

Dissolve gelatin in orange juice; set aside.

Combine 2 cups sugar and water in a medium-size stainless steel saucepan; cook over medium heat, stirring constantly, until sugar dissolves. Cover and continue to cook 2 to 3 minutes to wash down sugar crystals from sides of pan. Uncover; stir in gelatin mixture. Return to a boil; cook 20 minutes, stirring occasionally.

Remove from heat; let cool 15 minutes. Remove foam; add lemon extract, stirring well. Pour mixture into an 8-inch square pan that has been rinsed with water. Let stand overnight.

Sift together powdered sugar and cornstarch. Set aside.

Run a knife around edge of candy in pan; dip bottom of pan into hot water. Turn candy out onto a board that has been dusted with reserved cornstarch mixture. Turn candy over to coat both sides.

Cut candy into 1-inch squares, using scissors that have been coated with cornstarch mixture. Roll each piece in sugar mixture. Store in airtight containers with extra cornstarch mixture. Yield: about 5½ dozen.

STRAWBERRY TURKISH PASTE

1 (10-ounce) jar strawberry
  jam
1 (10-ounce) jar apple jelly
4 envelopes unflavored
  gelatin
¼ cup cold water
Sugar

Place an 8-inch square baking pan in refrigerator.

Combine strawberry jam and apple jelly in a medium saucepan; cook over medium-low heat, stirring constantly, until jelly mixture melts.

Dissolve gelatin in cold water; add to jam mixture, stirring well. Bring to a boil; boil 5 minutes, stirring constantly. Remove from heat, and pour into chilled baking pan. Let stand overnight.

Turn candy out onto a board that has been sprinkled with sugar; cut into 1-inch squares. Roll each square in sugar. Yield: about 5 dozen.

Note: Powdered sugar may be used instead of granulated.

ORIENTAL DELIGHT

6 envelopes unflavored
   gelatin
1 cup cold water, divided
2 cups sugar
½ cup light corn syrup
1 tablespoon lemon
   juice
⅓ cup orange juice
1 tablespoon finely chopped
   candied cherries
1 teaspoon vanilla
   extract
¼ cup plus 2 tablespoons
   powdered sugar
¼ cup cornstarch

Place a 13- x 9- x 2-inch baking pan in refrigerator until ready to use.

Combine gelatin and ¼ cup cold water in a small mixing bowl; set aside.

Combine 2 cups sugar, remaining water, syrup, and lemon juice in a small Dutch oven, stirring well. Bring to a boil; boil 5 minutes stirring constantly. Add reserved gelatin mixture, stirring well; cook, stirring constantly, until gelatin dissolves. Add orange juice and cherries; cook an additional 10 minutes, stirring well. Remove from heat; stir in vanilla. Pour mixture into chilled baking pan. Let stand overnight at room temperature.

Sift together powdered sugar and cornstarch; sprinkle mixture over counter top or on a baking sheet. Turn candy out onto cornstarch mixture. Cut into 1-inch squares. Roll each piece in cornstarch mixture; let dry on wire racks 1 hour. Store in airtight containers. Yield: about 10 dozen.

A couple is seen strolling through a banana "orchard" in this drawing by artist A. R. Waud, 1871.

Turkish paste as a form of candy probably predates the discovery of gelatin made of animal material. Agar, made from seaweed, is still used as a gel in Chinese cooking. Gum arabic (from the acacia) would have been available all over the Middle East. The earliest paste confections must have been sweetened with honey; fruit was available for flavor. Today, we may dip small cubes of paste into melted chocolate.

BANANA BITES

1 envelope unflavored gelatin
1 tablespoon plus 1½
   teaspoons cold water
2 tablespoons boiling water
2 cups sifted powdered sugar
¼ teaspoon banana extract
2 drops yellow food coloring

Dissolve gelatin in cold water in a medium mixing bowl; add boiling water, and stir until gelatin dissolves. Add sugar, mixing well. Cool slightly. Add banana extract and food coloring; knead until smooth and well blended.

Shape mixture into 1-inch balls; mold each ball into a banana. Yield: about 3 dozen.

TAFFY, DROPS, AND BRITTLES

TAFFY

2 cups sugar
¾ cup water
¼ cup vinegar
1 tablespoon plus 1½
teaspoons butter or
margarine
½ teaspoon vanilla extract

Combine sugar, water, vinegar, and butter in a 2-quart saucepan; cook over medium heat, stirring constantly, until sugar dissolves. Cover and continue to cook over medium heat 2 to 3 minutes to wash down sugar crystals from sides of pan. Uncover and cook, without stirring, until mixture reaches soft crack stage (270°). Remove from heat, and stir in vanilla.

Pour syrup into a well-buttered 15- x 10- x 1-inch jellyroll pan or onto a well-buttered marble slab. Allow syrup to cool slightly.

Work syrup into a mound, using a buttered spatula or candy scraper. Divide mound of candy in half. With buttered hands, pull, fold, and twist each portion until candy is opaque and begins to stiffen.

Pull each portion into a rope, ½-inch in diameter. Twist ropes together, forming 1 rope. Cut into 1-inch pieces; wrap each piece in waxed paper. Yield: about 2½ dozen.

Taffy evokes nostalgic memories — images of boardwalks, seaside resorts, and amusement parks come to mind. Even as children, we looked forward to our elders bringing back a bag of that tender, chewy confection. Wrapped in glassine and made by machine, it was delicious! Let's bring back the taffy-pulling party! The photographs at right show how to do it.

Taffy (left) and Kentucky Cream Candy (page 110); pulled to perfection.

HOW TO PULL TAFFY

Step 1 — Pick up one portion of candy with buttered hands. Pull into a rope. Fold ends together; twist and pull again.

Step 2 — Pull, fold, and twist 15 minutes or until candy is opaque, firm, and elastic. Pull into a rope, ½ inch in diameter.

Step 3 — Repeat procedure with remaining portion of candy. Twist ropes together, forming 1 rope.

Step 4 — Cut candy into 1-inch pieces, using well-buttered shears. Wrap each piece of candy in waxed paper.

SYRUP STAGES IN CANDY MAKING

A candy thermometer is a critical piece of equipment in candy making and should be used as a guide to determine the syrup stages. Always check the candy thermometer for accuracy before beginning a recipe. Place the thermometer in a pan of water. Bring the water to a boil. The thermometer should register 212°F. If the temperature reading is higher or lower than 212°F, take this difference into account when checking the temperature of the syrup.

However, the addition of other ingredients to the syrup, such as milk, butter, or honey, can affect the temperature of the syrup at different stages. It is then necessary to test the consistency of syrup by checking the visual and tactile characteristics of the syrups. Remove the syrup from the heat source while checking for the various stages to prevent overcooking the candy.

Thread Stage (230°-234°F) — Tip a teaspoonful of hot syrup over a dish. The syrup should form a fine, thin thread as it drips from the spoon. If syrup is too liquid, test again when temperature has increased by a few degrees.

Hard-Ball Stage (250°-268°F) — Pour a teaspoonful of hot syrup into a small bowl of ice water. Gather syrup into a ball. Remove ball from water. The ball should be resistant to pressure and hold its shape but still be pliable.

Soft-Crack Stage (270°-290°F) — Pour a teaspoonful of syrup into a small bowl of ice water. Gather syrup into a ball. Remove ball from water. The ball should separate into firm but elastic strands when stretched between fingers.

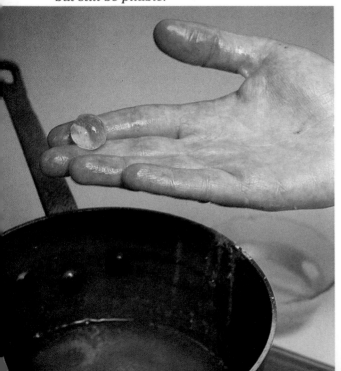

Soft-Ball Stage (234°-240°F) — Place a teaspoonful of hot syrup in a bowl of ice water. Using fingertips, gather syrup into a ball. Remove ball from water. The ball should flatten immediately and lose its shape.

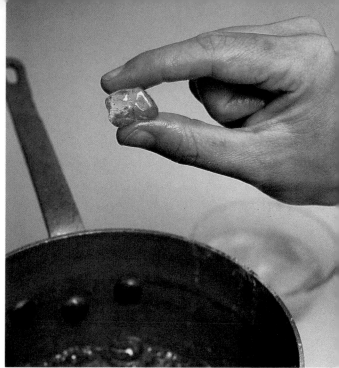

Firm-Ball Stage (242°-248°F) — Pour a teaspoonful of hot syrup into a small bowl of ice water. Gather syrup into a ball. Remove ball from water. The ball should be firm but pliable and retain its shape for a short period of time.

Hard-Crack Stage (300°-310°F) — Pour a teaspoonful of hot syrup into a small bowl of ice water. The syrup should harden immediately and separate into brittle threads. These threads will snap in two when removed from the water and bent.

Caramel Stage (310°-340°F) — Pour a teaspoonful of hot syrup onto a white plate. The syrup should be honey colored. Continued cooking will deepen the color and flavor of the caramel; at 350° it will turn black.

*Above: Young people at a
candy-pulling party.
Below: Taffy-pulling machine,
once a common sight.*

Brown Brothers

KENTUCKY CREAM CANDY

4 cups sugar
1 cup water
⅛ teaspoon baking soda
½ teaspoon salt
1 cup whipping cream

Combine sugar, water, soda, and salt in a large Dutch oven; cook over medium heat, stirring constantly, until sugar dissolves. Cover and continue to cook over medium heat 2 to 3 minutes to wash down sugar crystals from sides of pan. Uncover and cook, without stirring, until mixture reaches soft ball stage (234°).

Gradually add whipping cream, without stirring. Continue cooking over medium heat until mixture reaches hard ball stage (260°).

Remove from heat; pour mixture into a well-buttered 15- x 10- x 1-inch jellyroll pan. Allow mixture to cool slightly.

Work mixture into a mound, using a buttered spatula or candy scraper. Pick up mound with buttered hands; pull, fold, and twist until candy is opaque and begins to stiffen. Divide candy in half, and pull each half into a rope, ½-inch in diameter. Twist ropes together, and cut into 1-inch pieces. Wrap each piece in waxed paper. Yield: about 6 dozen.

Kentucky Cream Candy, although pulled like taffy, is not really taffy. Long a specialty of the state, it is marketed commercially and can be found in some gift shops. The candy, after being pulled until it holds ridges and begins to show slight crystallization, is cut with scissors and wrapped. Upon standing, crystallization is completed. Like the sugar and cream that it is, the candy simply melts in the mouth.

HOREHOUND CANDY

1½ quarts water
1 quart loosely packed horehound leaves and stems
3 cups sugar
1 teaspoon cream of tartar
1 teaspoon butter
1 teaspoon lemon juice

Combine water and horehound in a large saucepan. Bring to a boil. Reduce heat; simmer 30 minutes. Remove from heat; cover and steep 30 minutes. Strain; discard horehound, reserving liquid.

Combine liquid, sugar, and cream of tartar in a medium saucepan. Slowly bring to a boil, stirring until sugar dissolves. Cover and cook over medium heat 2 to 3 minutes to wash down sugar crystals from sides of pan. Uncover and cook, without stirring, until mixture reaches 220°; add butter (do not stir). Continue cooking, without stirring, until mixture reaches hard crack stage (300°). Add lemon juice (do not stir). Gently shake pan.

Quickly pour syrup into a buttered 15- x 10- x 1-inch jellyroll pan. Let cool slightly. Mark top of warm candy into 1-inch squares, using a sharp knife. Cool completely; break into squares. Wrap each square in waxed paper. Yield: 12½ dozen.

LOLLIPOPS

2 cups sugar
1 cup light corn syrup
½ cup water
1½ teaspoons peppermint oil
Red, green, and yellow food coloring

Cover 6 baking sheets with aluminum foil, and lightly grease each. Arrange 6 lollipop sticks in parallel rows on each sheet. Set aside.

Combine sugar, corn syrup, and water in a 2-quart saucepan; stir well. Cook over medium heat, stirring frequently, until sugar dissolves. Cover and continue to cook over medium heat 2 to 3 minutes to wash down sugar crystals from sides of pan. Uncover and cook, without stirring, until mixture reaches soft crack stage (275°). Remove from heat, and stir in peppermint oil. Pour syrup evenly into 3 small saucepans. Add 3 drops food coloring to each portion of syrup, using a different color in each. Stir well, and place each saucepan over low heat.

Working rapidly, with 1 portion at a time, drop hot syrup from tip of a tablespoon over alternate ends of lollipop sticks to form circles, 2 inches in diameter. Cool completely. Gently remove lollipops from aluminum foil, and wrap each tightly in plastic wrap or cellophane. Store in a cool, dry place. Yield: 3 dozen.

APPLE JACK STICKS

2 cups sugar
1 cup apple cider
1 teaspoon lemon juice

Combine sugar and apple cider in a medium saucepan. Slowly bring to a boil, stirring until sugar dissolves. Cover and cook over medium heat 2 to 3 minutes to wash down sugar crystals from sides of pan. Uncover and cook, without stirring, until mixture reaches soft crack stage (290°). Remove from heat; stir in lemon juice.

Drop syrup by teaspoonfuls onto waxed paper, keeping remaining syrup over low heat. Cool until set, and twist each candy into a stick. Place on a wire rack to cool completely. Wrap each stick in waxed paper. Yield: about 2½ dozen.

BLACK WALNUT BRITTLE

2 cups sugar
1 cup chopped black walnuts

Spread sugar evenly in a 10-inch cast-iron skillet. Cook over medium-low heat, stirring frequently, 30 minutes or until sugar turns light brown. Remove from heat; stir in walnuts.

Pour brittle into a buttered 15- x 10- x 1-inch jellyroll pan. Cool and break into pieces. Wrap in plastic wrap. Yield: about 1 pound.

Collection of Linda Campbell Franklin

PEANUT BRITTLE WREATH

2 cups sugar
¾ cup light corn syrup
¼ cup water
1¼ cups raw peanuts
2 teaspoons baking
　soda

Heavily grease a 12-inch round pizza pan and lower sides of a 46-ounce can. Place can, greased-side down, in center of pizza pan. Set aside.

Combine sugar, syrup, and water in a small Dutch oven. Cook over medium heat, stirring constantly, until sugar dissolves. Cover and continue to cook over medium heat 2 to 3 minutes to wash down sugar crystals from sides of pan. Uncover; add peanuts. Continue to cook over medium heat, stirring constantly, until mixture reaches soft crack stage (275°).

Remove from heat, and stir in soda. Beat mixture constantly with a wooden spoon until golden in color. Quickly spread mixture on prepared pizza pan, and press to fit around can.

Cool slightly; carefully remove can from center. Allow peanut brittle to cool completely before removing from pan. Wrap in plastic wrap. Yield: one 12-inch wreath.

PECAN CRUNCH

2 cups sugar
1 tablespoon butter
2 cups coarsely ground
　pecans

Combine sugar and butter in a 10-inch cast-iron skillet; cook over medium heat, stirring constantly, until sugar dissolves and becomes a golden syrup.

Remove from heat; stir in ground pecans. Working rapidly, pour mixture into a buttered 8-inch square pan. Mark top of warm candy into 1-inch squares, using a sharp knife. Cool completely before breaking into squares. Store in an airtight container. Yield: about 5 dozen.

Note: Ground walnuts or peanuts may be used in place of ground pecans.

PECAN BRITTLE

1 cup sugar
½ cup light corn syrup
¼ cup hot water
1 cup chopped pecans
1 tablespoon butter or
　margarine
1 teaspoon baking soda

Combine sugar, syrup, and water in a 2-quart saucepan. Cook over medium heat, stirring constantly, until sugar dissolves. Cover and cook 2 to 3 minutes to wash down sugar crystals from sides of pan. Uncover and cook, without stirring, until mixture reaches thread stage (230°). Add pecans; continue to cook, stirring constantly, until mixture reaches hard crack stage (300°).

Remove from heat; stir in butter and soda, mixing well. Working rapidly, spread mixture in a buttered 9-inch square baking pan. Cool; break into pieces. Yield: about 1 pound.

A complementary team: candymakers and taste testers at work, 1890s trade card for extracts.

KELLOGG'S EXTRACTS
FOR CARAMELS AND ALL CANDIES.

CHOCOLATE-PECAN BRITTLE

1 cup sugar
⅓ cup light corn syrup
⅓ cup water
⅛ teaspoon salt
2 (1-ounce) squares
   semisweet chocolate, grated
⅔ cup chopped pecans

Combine sugar, syrup, water, and salt in a 2-quart saucepan. Cook over medium heat, stirring constantly, until sugar dissolves. Cover and continue to cook over medium heat 2 to 3 minutes to wash down sugar crystals from sides of pan. Uncover and cook, without stirring, until mixture reaches soft crack stage (280°).

Remove from heat; add chocolate and pecans. Beat constantly with a wooden spoon until mixture begins to thicken. Working rapidly, spread mixture evenly in a thin layer on a buttered baking sheet. Cool completely; break into pieces. Store candy in an airtight container, or wrap in plastic wrap. Yield: about 2 pounds.

COCONUT BRITTLE

1 cup firmly packed brown
   sugar
1 cup light corn syrup
1 tablespoon butter or
   margarine
1 teaspoon vinegar
1½ cups grated coconut

Combine sugar, syrup, butter, and vinegar in a 2-quart saucepan. Cook over medium heat, stirring constantly, until sugar dissolves. Cover and cook 2 to 3 minutes to wash down sugar crystals from sides of pan. Uncover and cook, without stirring, until mixture reaches hard crack stage (300°).

Remove from heat; stir in coconut. Spread mixture evenly in a buttered baking sheet. Cool completely; break into pieces. Store in an airtight container. Yield: about 1 pound.

The Cumberland, Maryland, Mid-Summer Festival of 1909 featured The Candy Kid booth among others.

More than any other candy, excepting fondant, brittles benefit from being poured out onto marble. Quick cooling is of the essence, and the absence of pan sides allows the candymaker to pick up the edges as soon as the candy cools a little and stretch it to make a thinner, more delicate product. Note that when the soda is added to straight brittles, the mixture foams up. This "brittle rising" makes a more tender, chewable candy; otherwise it would have the consistency of a lollipop. Brittles always find their place, plastic bagged and ribboned, under many a Christmas tree!

POPCORN BALLS

12 cups freshly popped
    popcorn, salted
1 cup sugar
1 cup molasses
2 tablespoons butter or
    margarine
1 tablespoon vinegar
½ teaspoon baking soda

Place popcorn in a lightly greased large mixing bowl; set aside.

Combine sugar, molasses, butter, and vinegar in a small Dutch oven. Bring to a boil, stirring until sugar dissolves. Cover and continue to cook over medium heat 2 to 3 minutes to wash down sugar crystals from sides of pan. Uncover and cook, without stirring, until mixture reaches hard ball stage (250°).

Remove from heat; stir in soda. Pour syrup over reserved popcorn; stir until all popcorn is coated. Cool slightly, and shape into 3-inch balls. Yield: 2 dozen.

"Get your Cracker Jack here" has been the cry at circuses and ball games since 1896, when the Rueckheim brothers of Chicago added molasses and peanuts to the native Indian popcorn. Popcorn balls with molasses were already being eaten at the time. Holiday idea: make a clear syrup for a Christmas snowman; color it red for ornaments or green for a tree. For 12 cups popped corn, cook 1 cup sugar, 1 cup white corn syrup, and ½ cup water to 240°. (Method as in Popcorn Balls.) Stir in 2 tablespoons butter, 2 teaspoons vanilla, and food coloring, if desired. Mix with warm popcorn; mold into shapes.

CRACKER JACKS

¾ cup unpopped popcorn
1 cup firmly packed brown
    sugar
½ cup butter or margarine
¼ cup light corn syrup
¼ cup molasses
½ teaspoon salt
½ teaspoon baking soda
1 cup raw peanuts,
    toasted

Pop popcorn, and place in a lightly greased 15- x 10- x 1-inch jellyroll pan. Set aside.

Combine sugar, butter, syrup, molasses, and salt in a large saucepan. Bring to a boil; boil 5 minutes, stirring constantly. Remove from heat; stir in soda and peanuts.

Pour hot syrup over popcorn in prepared pan, stirring until evenly coated. Bake at 200° for 1 hour, stirring every 15 minutes to separate pieces. Cool and store in an airtight container. Yield: about 4 quarts.

Popcorn Balls and Cracker Jacks, perennial favorites.

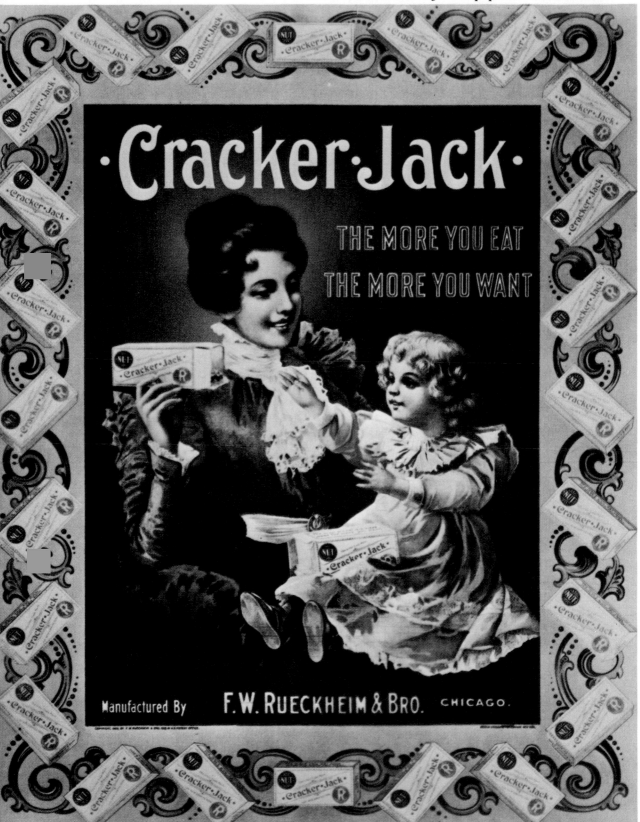

BUTTERSCOTCH AND CARAMELS

PECAN TOFFEE

2 cups butter
2 cups sugar
¼ cup plus 2 tablespoons
water
2 cups coarsely chopped
pecans
1 (12-ounce) package
semisweet chocolate
morsels

Melt butter in a 3-quart saucepan over medium heat. Add sugar and water, stirring until sugar dissolves. Cook over medium heat, without stirring, until mixture reaches soft crack stage (295°).

Remove from heat; quickly add pecans, stirring well. Pour mixture into an aluminum foil-lined 15- x 10- x 1-inch jellyroll pan. Let cool.

Melt chocolate morsels in top of a double boiler over simmering water. Spread chocolate over toffee. Cover and refrigerate until completely cooled and hardened. Break into pieces. Store in an airtight container. Yield: about 3 pounds.

BUTTERSCOTCH SUCKERS

2 cups firmly packed brown
sugar
¼ cup water
2 tablespoons vinegar
½ cup butter or margarine
½ teaspoon vanilla extract

Arrange 24 wooden sticks on well-buttered baking pans, and set aside.

Combine sugar, water, vinegar, and butter in a 2-quart saucepan. Cook over medium heat, stirring constantly, until sugar dissolves. Cover and continue to cook over medium heat 2 to 3 minutes to wash down sugar crystals from sides of pan. Uncover and cook, without stirring, until mixture reaches hard ball stage (260°). Remove from heat, and stir in vanilla.

Immediately drop mixture by tablespoonfuls onto alternate ends of each wooden stick. Allow suckers to cool completely before removing from pans. Wrap each sucker tightly in plastic wrap. Yield: 2 dozen.

MOLASSES CARAMELS

1 cup molasses
1 cup sugar
½ cup butter or margarine

Combine all ingredients in a 2-quart saucepan. Cook over medium heat, stirring constantly, until butter melts and sugar dissolves. Cover and continue to cook over medium heat 2 to 3 minutes to wash down sugar crystals from sides of pan. Uncover and cook, without stirring, until mixture reaches hard ball stage (260°).

Remove from heat, and beat with a wooden spoon until mixture is creamy and begins to thicken. Working rapidly, spread mixture in a buttered 8-inch square pan. Mark top of warm candy into 1-inch squares, using a sharp knife. Cool completely before cutting into squares. Wrap each piece tightly in waxed paper or plastic wrap. Yield: about 5 dozen.

Working on an all-day sucker, c.1920.

Brown Brothers

Toffees, caramels, and butterscotches have their differences, although they use similar ingredients. The high butter content in toffee makes it agreeably chewable; cooking it to the soft crack stage gives it the crunch. The soft, chewy texture of caramel is achieved by cooking the syrup to a lower stage than that of toffee—firm ball or hard ball. After pouring out caramel, keep going over the cut lines to keep the squares sharp. Wrap the cut squares tightly to retain the perfect shape. The combination of brown sugar and butter gives butterscotch its distinctive flavor.

Natty bears with peppermint sticks on a candy label, 1898.

CREAMY PECAN CARAMELS

2 cups sugar
1 cup firmly packed brown sugar
1 cup light corn syrup
¾ cup butter
1 cup whipping cream
1 tablespoon plus 1 teaspoon vanilla extract
4 cups coarsely chopped pecans

Combine sugar, syrup, butter, and whipping cream in a large Dutch oven. Cook over medium heat, stirring constantly, until sugar dissolves. Cover and continue to cook over medium heat 2 to 3 minutes to wash down sugar crystals from sides of pan. Uncover and cook, stirring frequently, until mixture reaches firm ball stage (244°).

Remove from heat. Stir in vanilla and pecans, mixing well. Working rapidly, spread mixture in a buttered 15- x 10- x 1-inch jellyroll pan. Cool completely before cutting into 1-inch squares. Wrap each piece in plastic wrap. Store in airtight containers. Yield: 12½ dozen.

CARAMELTS

2¾ cups sugar, divided
1 cup light corn syrup
1½ cups evaporated milk, divided
¼ cup plus 2 tablespoons butter, divided
1 teaspoon vanilla extract
⅛ teaspoon baking soda
1 tablespoon cooking sherry

Combine 1 cup sugar, syrup, 1 cup milk, and 2 tablespoons butter in a small Dutch oven; cook over low heat, stirring constantly, until sugar dissolves. Continue to cook over medium heat, stirring frequently, until mixture reaches firm ball stage (244°). Remove from heat; add vanilla, stirring well. Place Dutch oven in hot water to keep mixture warm.

Place ½ cup sugar in a 10-inch cast-iron skillet; cook over medium heat, stirring constantly, until sugar dissolves and becomes a golden syrup.

Combine remaining 1¼ cups sugar, remaining ½ cup milk, and soda in a small Dutch oven; bring to a boil, stirring constantly. Add caramelized sugar, stirring well. Cook, stirring frequently, until mixture reaches soft ball stage (234°). Remove from heat, and stir in remaining ¼ cup butter and sherry; add reserved warm mixture, and beat at medium speed of an electric mixer until thickened.

Pour mixture into a well-buttered 9-inch square baking pan. Cool completely before cutting into ½-inch squares; wrap each piece tightly in plastic wrap or waxed paper. Yield: 27 dozen.

CHOCOLATE CARAMELS

4 (1-ounce) squares
  unsweetened chocolate
1 cup milk
1 cup firmly packed brown
  sugar
1 cup light corn syrup
1 tablespoon butter
1 teaspoon vanilla
  extract

Combine chocolate and milk in a small Dutch oven; cook over low heat, stirring until chocolate melts. Add sugar and syrup; continue cooking, stirring constantly, until sugar dissolves and mixture comes to a boil. Cover and cook over medium heat 2 to 3 minutes to wash down sugar crystals from sides of pan. Uncover and cook, stirring occasionally, until mixture reaches thread stage (230°). Stir in butter and vanilla. Continue cooking until mixture reaches soft ball stage (236°).

Remove from heat, and cool to lukewarm (110°). Shape mixture into ropes, ⅜-inch in diameter; cut each rope into 1½-inch pieces. Wrap each piece in plastic wrap or waxed paper. Yield: about 5 dozen.

Chocolate, Creamy Pecan (page 117), and Ribbon caramels.

RIBBON CARAMELS

1¼ cups sugar
1½ cups light corn syrup,
  divided
1¼ cups whipping cream
¼ cup butter or margarine
Pinch of cream of tartar
2 (1-ounce) squares
  semisweet chocolate, grated
1 teaspoon vanilla extract
⅔ cup sugar
¼ cup water
2¼ cups flaked coconut

Combine 1¼ cups sugar, ½ cup syrup, whipping cream, butter, and cream of tartar in a 2-quart saucepan. Cook over medium heat, stirring until sugar dissolves. Cover and continue to cook over medium heat 2 to 3 minutes to wash down sugar crystals from sides of pan. Uncover and cook, stirring occasionally, until mixture reaches firm ball stage (244°).

Remove from heat, and stir in grated chocolate and vanilla. Beat constantly with a wooden spoon until mixture is thick and creamy. Working rapidly, spread mixture evenly in two buttered 8-inch square baking pans. Mark top of warm candy into 1-inch squares, using a sharp knife. Set aside to cool completely.

Combine ⅔ cup sugar, remaining syrup, and water in a 2-quart saucepan. Cook over medium heat, stirring constantly, until sugar dissolves. Cover and continue to cook over medium heat 2 to 3 minutes to wash down sugar crystals from sides of pan. Uncover and cook, without stirring, until mixture reaches firm ball stage (244°). Remove from heat, and stir in coconut.

Working rapidly, spread mixture evenly over top of chocolate mixture in one of the pans. Carefully remove remaining chocolate layer from other pan, and press, bottom side down, firmly on top of coconut mixture. Cool completely before cutting into 1-inch squares. Wrap each piece of candy tightly in plastic wrap or waxed paper. Yield: about 5 dozen.

Children around the hearth after a visit from Santa Claus, 1922.

HOLIDAY DELIGHT LOGS

3 cups sugar
1 cup light corn syrup
1½ cups half-and-half
1½ teaspoons vanilla extract
½ pound candied cherries,
   coarsely chopped
½ pound candied pineapple,
   coarsely chopped
1¾ cups chopped pecans
1¾ cups chopped walnuts
1¾ cups chopped Brazil nuts

Combine sugar, syrup, and half-and-half in a 3-quart saucepan. Bring to a boil, stirring until sugar dissolves. Cook over medium heat, stirring occasionally, until mixture reaches soft ball stage (238°).

Remove from heat; beat at medium speed of an electric mixer 8 minutes or until mixture thickens. Stir in vanilla, candied fruit, and nuts. With buttered hands, divide mixture into 7 equal portions. Shape each portion into an 8-inch log. Wrap each log in waxed paper; chill thoroughly. Remove waxed paper, and cut each log into ¼-inch-thick slices. Store in airtight containers in refrigerator. Yield: about 19 dozen.

FUDGES AND PRALINES

COLLEGE FUDGE

1 cup sugar
1 cup firmly packed brown sugar
½ cup whipping cream
¼ cup molasses
¼ cup butter
1½ teaspoons vanilla extract

Combine sugar, whipping cream, and molasses in a small Dutch oven; cook over medium heat, stirring constantly, until sugar dissolves and mixture comes to a boil. Cover and continue to cook over medium heat 2 to 3 minutes to wash down sugar crystals from sides of pan. Uncover and cook, stirring occasionally, until mixture reaches soft ball stage (238°).

Remove from heat; add butter and vanilla (do not stir). Cool to lukewarm (110°). Beat with a wooden spoon until mixture thickens and begins to lose its gloss; pour into a buttered 8-inch square baking pan. Cut into 1-inch squares. Yield: about 5 dozen.

Cover of recipe booklet published by the Franklin Sugar Company, c.1910.

Collection of Bonnie Slotnick

QUICK FUDGE

3 (1-ounce) squares unsweetened chocolate
¼ cup butter
1 (16-ounce) package powdered sugar, sifted
¼ cup evaporated milk
½ cup chopped pecans
1 teaspoon vanilla extract
⅛ teaspoon salt

Melt chocolate and butter in top of a double boiler over simmering water, stirring well.

Remove from heat. Add sugar and milk; stir until well blended. Add pecans, vanilla, and salt; mix well. Press mixture into a buttered 8-inch square baking pan. Chill and cut into 1-inch squares. Store in airtight containers. Yield: about 5 dozen.

CHOCOLATE FUDGE

4 cups sugar
1½ cups milk
2 (1-ounce) squares unsweetened chocolate, grated
¼ cup butter or margarine
1 teaspoon vanilla extract

Combine sugar, milk, and grated chocolate in a large Dutch oven. Cook over medium heat, stirring constantly, until sugar dissolves. Cover and continue to cook over medium heat 2 to 3 minutes to wash down sugar crystals from sides of pan. Uncover and cook, stirring occasionally, until mixture reaches soft ball stage (234°).

Remove from heat; add butter and vanilla (do not stir). Cool to lukewarm (110°). Beat until mixture thickens and begins to lose its gloss. Working rapidly, spread mixture in a buttered 9-inch square baking pan. Cut candy into 1-inch squares. Store in airtight containers. Yield: about 7 dozen.

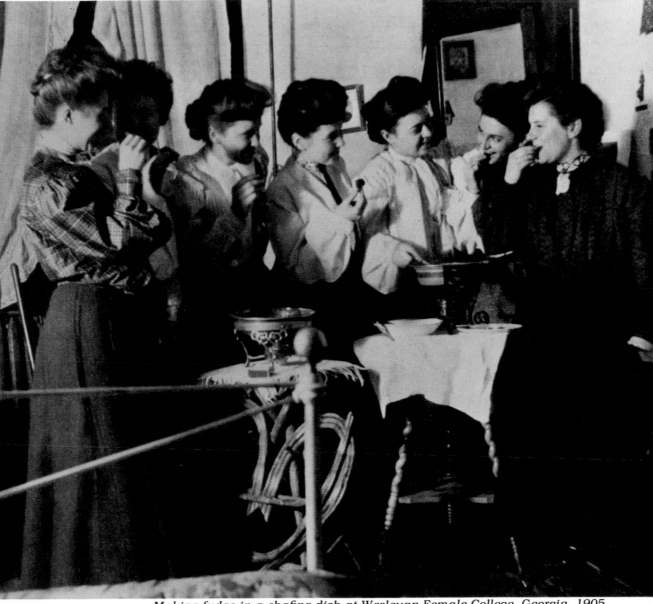

Making fudge in a chafing dish at Wesleyan Female College, Georgia, 1905.

FAVORITE CHOCOLATE FUDGE

2 cups sugar
2 cups firmly packed brown sugar
4 (1-ounce) squares unsweetened chocolate, grated
2 (5.33-ounce) cans evaporated milk
¼ cup butter
2 teaspoons vanilla extract

Combine sugar, grated chocolate, and milk in a large Dutch oven; cook over medium heat, stirring constantly, until sugar dissolves. Cover and continue to cook over medium heat 2 to 3 minutes to wash down sugar crystals from sides of pan. Uncover and cook, stirring occasionally, until mixture reaches soft ball stage (236°).

Remove from heat; add butter and vanilla (do not stir). Let stand 15 minutes or until mixture cools to lukewarm (110°). Beat with a wooden spoon until mixture thickens and begins to lose its gloss.

Working rapidly, spread mixture in a buttered 9-inch square baking pan. Mark top of warm candy into 1½-inch squares, using a sharp knife. Cool completely before cutting. Store in an airtight container. Yield: 3 dozen.

ANGEL FUDGE

4 cups sugar
2 cups milk
1 cup chocolate-flavored
  syrup
2 tablespoons butter
2 teaspoons vanilla
  extract
1 (7-ounce) jar marshmallow
  creme

Combine sugar, milk, and chocolate syrup in a 3-quart saucepan. Cook over medium heat, stirring constantly, until sugar dissolves. Cover and continue to cook over medium heat 2 to 3 minutes to wash down sugar crystals from sides of pan. Uncover and cook, stirring occasionally, until mixture reaches soft ball stage (236°).

Remove from heat; add butter, vanilla, and marshmallow creme (do not stir). Cool to lukewarm (110°). Beat with a wooden spoon until mixture thickens. Pour into a buttered 13- x 9- x 2-inch baking pan. Cool and cut into 1-inch squares. Yield: about 10 dozen.

Young cooks are finishing up a batch of fudge in this illustration from The Fun of Cooking, *1915.*

DARK CHOCOLATE
FUDGE

3 tablespoons butter
3 cups sugar
1 (5.33-ounce) can evaporated
  milk
¼ cup light corn syrup
Dash of salt
3 (1-ounce) squares
  unsweetened chocolate
1 teaspoon vanilla extract

Brown butter lightly in a 3-quart saucepan. Add sugar, milk, syrup, and salt; stir well. Cook over medium heat, stirring constantly, until sugar dissolves. Stir in chocolate. Cover and continue to cook 2 to 3 minutes to wash down sugar crystals from sides of pan. Uncover and cook, stirring occasionally, until mixture reaches soft ball stage (240°).

Remove from heat. Cool to lukewarm (110°). Add vanilla; beat with a wooden spoon until mixture thickens and begins to cool. Pour into a buttered 9-inch square baking pan. Cool and cut into 1½-inch squares. Yield: about 3 dozen.

Note: ½ cup peanut butter may be stirred into chocolate mixture just before removing from heat.

CHOCOLATE-PECAN
FUDGE

2 cups sugar
2 (1-ounce) squares
  unsweetened chocolate
½ cup milk
⅓ cup light corn syrup
¼ cup butter or margarine
Dash of salt
1 cup chopped pecans
1½ teaspoons vanilla extract

Combine sugar, chocolate, milk, syrup, butter, and salt in a 10-inch cast-iron skillet. Bring to a boil, stirring constantly. Boil 2 minutes or until mixture reaches soft ball stage (236°).

Remove from heat; add pecans and vanilla (do not stir). Cool to lukewarm (110°). Beat with a wooden spoon until mixture is thick and creamy. Pour into a buttered 8-inch square baking pan. Cool completely before cutting into 1-inch squares. Yield: about 5 dozen.

FESTIVE FUDGE

2 cups sugar
½ cup butter or margarine
12 large marshmallows
1 (5.33-ounce) can evaporated
  milk
Dash of salt
1 (6-ounce) package
  semisweet chocolate
  morsels
1 cup chopped pecans
1½ teaspoons vanilla extract

Combine sugar, butter, marshmallows, milk, and salt in a large heavy saucepan. Cook over medium heat, stirring constantly, until sugar dissolves. Cover and continue to cook over medium heat 2 to 3 minutes to wash down sugar crystals from sides of pan. Uncover and cook, stirring occasionally, 5 minutes or until mixture reaches soft ball stage (236°).

Remove from heat; add chocolate, stirring until melted. Stir in pecans and vanilla. Spread in a buttered 8-inch square baking dish. Cool completely; cut into 1½-inch squares. Yield: about 3 dozen.

Collection of Bonnie Slotnick

Festive Fudge (below) and Orange Fudge (page 124)

COCONUT FUDGE

3 cups sugar
2 (1-ounce) squares
  unsweetened chocolate,
  grated
1½ cups milk
2 tablespoons butter
½ teaspoon vanilla extract
1½ cups flaked coconut,
  chopped

Combine sugar, grated chocolate, milk, and butter in a large Dutch oven; cook over medium heat, stirring constantly, until sugar dissolves. Cover and continue to cook over medium heat 2 to 3 minutes to wash down sugar crystals from sides of pan. Uncover and cook, stirring occasionally, until mixture reaches soft ball stage (234°).

Remove from heat; let stand 15 minutes or until mixture cools to lukewarm (110°). Do not stir. Add vanilla and coconut; beat mixture with a wooden spoon until mixture thickens and begins to lose its gloss.

Working rapidly, spread mixture into a buttered 9-inch square baking pan. Mark top of warm candy into 1½-inch squares, using a sharp knife. Cool completely before cutting into squares. Store in an airtight container. Yield: about 3 dozen.

ORANGE FUDGE

2 cups sugar
¾ cup milk
2 tablespoons light corn
  syrup
1 tablespoon butter
1 tablespoon grated orange
  rind
2 tablespoons orange juice
1 tablespoon orange extract

Combine sugar, milk, syrup, butter, and orange rind in a medium-size non-aluminum saucepan. Cook over medium heat, stirring constantly, until sugar dissolves. Cover and continue to cook over medium heat 2 to 3 minutes to wash down sugar crystals from sides of pan. Uncover and cook, stirring frequently, until mixture reaches soft ball stage (238°).

Remove from heat; cool to lukewarm (110°). Add orange juice and extract. Beat with a wooden spoon 2 to 3 minutes or until fudge thickens and begins to lose its gloss.

Pour fudge into a buttered 8-inch square baking pan. Mark top of warm candy into 1-inch squares, using a sharp knife. Cool completely before cutting. Store in airtight containers. Yield: about 5 dozen.

In studying an assortment of homemade candies, some of us look for telltale signs of coconut, even under a chocolate coating. Packages of shredded or flaked coconut are so easy to come by now that we rarely find time to prepare it fresh. We use more flaked coconut than shredded, mostly because it doesn't tear the finished product when cut. But if we decide to make old-fashioned "haystacks" out of that Coconut Fudge, we use shredded coconut and drop it from a spoon into shaggy cone shapes.

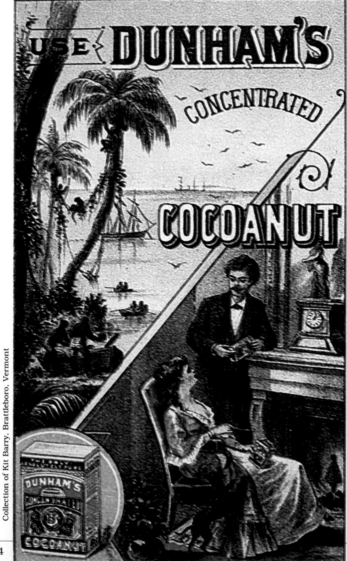

Trade card with two scenes of serenity, c.1885.

Collection of Kit Barry, Brattleboro, Vermont

PEANUT BUTTER FUDGE

3 cups sugar
1 cup milk
½ cup butter
½ teaspoon salt
3 tablespoons peanut butter
1 teaspoon vanilla extract

Combine sugar, milk, butter, and salt in a small Dutch oven; cook over medium heat, stirring constantly, until sugar dissolves. Cover and continue to cook over medium heat 2 to 3 minutes to wash down sugar crystals from sides of pan. Uncover and cook, without stirring, until mixture reaches soft ball stage (236°).

Remove from heat, and stir in peanut butter and vanilla. Beat at medium speed of an electric mixer until fudge begins to harden; pour into a buttered 8-inch square baking pan. Mark top of warm candy into 1-inch squares, using a sharp knife. Cool completely before cutting. Yield: about 5 dozen.

A fudge-making scene introduced a Karo booklet, c.1910.

BLOND PECAN FUDGE

2 cups sugar
1 (5.33-ounce) can evaporated milk
1 egg
¼ cup butter
1 teaspoon vanilla extract
1 cup chopped pecans

Combine sugar, milk, egg, and butter in a medium-size heavy saucepan. Cook over medium heat, stirring constantly, until sugar dissolves. Cover and continue to cook 2 to 3 minutes to wash down sugar crystals from sides of pan. Uncover and cook, stirring frequently 20 minutes or until mixture reaches soft ball stage (234°).

Remove from heat. Cool to lukewarm (110°). Stir in vanilla and pecans; beat until mixture thickens slightly. Pour into a buttered 8-inch square baking pan. Cool slightly; cut fudge into 1½-inch squares. Store in airtight containers. Yield: about 3 dozen.

SOUR CREAM FUDGE

2 cups sugar
⅓ cup light corn syrup
⅓ cup sour cream
2 tablespoons butter
¼ teaspoon salt
2 teaspoons vanilla extract
1 cup chopped pecans
¼ cup red candied cherries, coarsely chopped

Combine sugar, syrup, sour cream, butter, and salt in a medium-size heavy saucepan; cook over medium heat, stirring constantly, until sugar dissolves. Cover and continue to cook over medium heat 2 to 3 minutes to wash down sugar crystals from sides of pan. Uncover and cook, without stirring, until mixture reaches soft ball stage (236°).

Remove from heat, and let stand, without stirring, 15 minutes or until mixture cools to lukewarm (110°). Add vanilla, chopped pecans, and cherries; beat with a wooden spoon until mixture thickens and begins to lose its gloss. Working rapidly, spread mixture in a buttered 8-inch square baking pan. Mark top of warm candy into 1-inch squares, using a sharp knife. Cool completely before cutting into squares. Store in airtight containers in a cool place. Yield: about 5 dozen.

President Street Penuche (front); Mexican Sweet Potato Candy.

Penuche, sometimes called panocha, is an old-fashioned fudge from Mexico. At least one member in every family prefers its light color and faint caramel flavor over chocolate. The use of dark or light brown sugar is a matter of personal preference, depending upon how pronounced a flavor is desired. Note that in many candies, white corn syrup is used. It helps to prevent the formation of large sugar crystals in finished candy.

PRESIDENT STREET PENUCHE

1½ cups sugar
¾ cup firmly packed brown sugar
¾ cup milk
1 tablespoon light corn syrup
1 tablespoon butter or margarine
⅛ teaspoon salt
1 teaspoon vanilla extract
1 cup chopped pecans

Combine sugar, milk, syrup, butter, and salt in a small Dutch oven. Cook over medium heat, stirring constantly, until sugar dissolves. Cover and cook 2 to 3 minutes to wash down sugar crystals from sides of pan. Uncover and cook, without stirring, until mixture reaches soft ball stage (234°).

Remove from heat (do not stir). Cool to lukewarm (110°). Add vanilla and pecans; beat with a wooden spoon 2 to 3 minutes or until mixture thickens and begins to lose its gloss.

Working rapidly, spread mixture in a buttered 8-inch square baking pan. Mark top of warm candy into 1½-inch squares, using a sharp knife. Cool completely before cutting. Store in an airtight container. Yield: about 2 dozen.

RAISIN PENUCHE

3 cups firmly packed light brown sugar
1 cup milk
½ cup butter
1 teaspoon vanilla extract
½ cup chopped walnuts
½ cup raisins

Combine sugar, milk, and butter in a medium Dutch oven. Cook over medium heat, stirring constantly, until sugar dissolves. Cover and continue to cook over medium heat 2 to 3 minutes to wash down sugar crystals from sides of pan. Uncover and cook, without stirring, until mixture reaches soft ball stage (234°).

Remove from heat (do not stir). Cool to lukewarm (110°). Add vanilla, walnuts, and raisins; beat at medium speed of an electric mixer until mixture thickens and begins to lose its gloss. Working rapidly, spread mixture in a buttered 8-inch square baking pan. Mark top of warm candy into 1-inch squares, using a sharp knife. Cool completely before cutting. Yield: about 5 dozen.

126

MEXICAN SWEET POTATO CANDY

2 cups firmly packed brown
sugar
¾ cup evaporated milk
1 tablespoon butter or
margarine
⅛ teaspoon salt
½ cup mashed, cooked sweet
potatoes
½ cup chopped pecans

Combine sugar, milk, butter, and salt in a 2-quart saucepan. Cook over low heat, stirring until sugar dissolves. Wash off sugar crystals that have formed on sides of pan, using a brush dipped in cold water.

Continue to cook, stirring occasionally, until mixture reaches firm ball stage (244°).

Remove from heat; cool to lukewarm (110°). Add sweet potatoes; beat at medium speed of an electric mixer until mixture thickens. Stir in pecans. Pour candy into a well-buttered large serving platter. Cool and cut into 1-inch squares. Yield: about 5 dozen.

CREOLE PRALINES

3 cups coarsely chopped
pecans
3 cups sugar
1½ cups milk
¼ cup light corn syrup
2 tablespoons butter or
margarine
1 tablespoon vanilla extract

Combine pecans, sugar, milk, and syrup in a small Dutch oven; mix well. Slowly bring to a boil, stirring constantly, until sugar dissolves. Cover and cook 2 to 3 minutes to wash down sugar crystals from sides of pan. Uncover and cook, without stirring, until mixture reaches soft ball stage (234°).

Remove from heat, and add butter, without stirring. Let cool to room temperature. Add vanilla; beat with a wooden spoon until mixture is creamy and begins to thicken.

Working rapidly, drop mixture by rounded tablespoonfuls onto waxed paper. Let cool. Yield: about 3½ dozen.

A Mexican market scene, painted by an unknown Mexican artist, c.1775.

GEORGIA NUGGETS

3 cups firmly packed brown
  sugar
⅛ teaspoon salt
1 cup whipping cream
1½ tablespoons butter
½ teaspoon vanilla
  extract
2 cups coarsely chopped
  pecans

Combine sugar, salt, and whipping cream in a 4-quart Dutch oven; cook over medium heat, stirring constantly, until sugar dissolves. Cover and continue to cook over medium heat 2 to 3 minutes to wash down sugar crystals from sides of pan. Uncover and cook, stirring occasionally, until mixture reaches soft ball stage (234°).

Remove from heat, and add butter (do not stir). Let stand 15 minutes or until mixture cools to lukewarm (110°). Add vanilla and pecans; beat mixture with a wooden spoon until mixture thickens and begins to lose its gloss.

Working rapidly, drop mixture by tablespoonfuls onto buttered waxed paper. Cool completely. Remove from waxed paper, and store in airtight containers. Yield: about 4½ dozen.

BUTTERMILK PRALINES

3 cups sugar
1 cup buttermilk
1 teaspoon cream of tartar
3 tablespoons butter
1½ teaspoons vanilla extract
2 cups coarsely chopped
  pecans

Combine sugar and buttermilk in a small Dutch oven, mixing well. Slowly bring to a boil, stirring constantly, until sugar dissolves. Cover and cook 2 to 3 minutes to wash down sugar crystals from sides of pan. Uncover and cook, stirring occasionally, until mixture reaches soft ball stage (234°). Stir in cream of tartar.

Remove from heat; stir in butter and vanilla. Beat 2 to 3 minutes or until mixture is creamy and begins to thicken. Stir in pecans. Working rapidly, drop mixture by rounded tablespoonfuls onto waxed paper; let cool. Remove from waxed paper, and store in an airtight container. Yield: about 1½ dozen.

PLANTATION PRALINES

1 cup sugar
1 cup firmly packed brown
  sugar
1 (8-ounce) carton
  commercial sour cream
2 tablespoons light corn
  syrup
Dash of salt
2 tablespoons butter or
  margarine
1 tablespoon vanilla extract
1½ cups pecan pieces

Combine sugar, sour cream, syrup, and salt in a medium-size heavy saucepan. Slowly bring to a boil, stirring constantly, until sugar dissolves. Cover and continue to cook 2 to 3 minutes to wash down sugar crystals from sides of pan. Uncover and cook, stirring occasionally, until mixture reaches soft ball stage (234°).

Remove from heat; stir in butter and vanilla. Beat with a wooden spoon until mixture is creamy and begins to thicken. Stir in pecans. Quickly drop candy by rounded tablespoonfuls onto waxed paper; let cool. Remove from waxed paper, and store in an airtight container. Yield: about 2 dozen.

Cross Roads syrup label from Cairo, Georgia, c.1910.

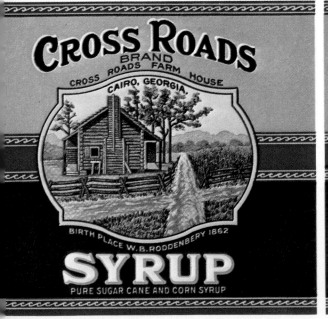

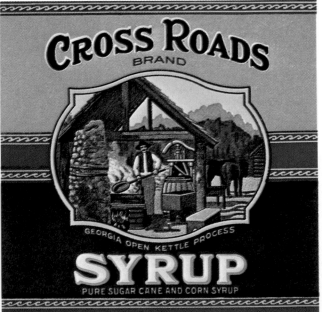

Plantation Pralines (below) and Peanut Patties (page 130)

MAPLE PRALINES

1 teaspoon vinegar
⅔ cup milk
2 cups sugar
1 cup maple syrup
2 cups chopped walnuts

Combine vinegar and milk in a small Dutch oven, stirring well; add sugar and syrup, stirring well. Slowly bring to a boil, stirring until sugar dissolves. Cover and continue to cook over medium heat 2 to 3 minutes to wash down sugar crystals from sides of pan. Uncover and continue cooking, stirring occasionally, until mixture reaches soft ball stage (232°).

Remove from heat, and cool to lukewarm (110°). Beat with a wooden spoon until mixture is creamy and begins to thicken; stir in walnuts. Working rapidly, drop mixture by tablespoonfuls onto waxed paper; let cool. Store in airtight containers. Yield: about 3 dozen.

COCONUT PRALINES

2 cups sugar
Dash of salt
½ cup fresh coconut milk
2 cups shredded fresh
   coconut
½ teaspoon vanilla extract

Combine sugar, salt, and coconut milk in a 2-quart saucepan. Cook over medium heat, stirring constantly, until sugar dissolves. Cover and continue to cook 2 to 3 minutes to wash down sugar crystals from sides of pan. Uncover and cook, without stirring, until mixture reaches soft ball stage (234°). Stir in coconut; return mixture to soft ball stage.

Remove from heat. Let cool 10 minutes. Stir in vanilla. Beat with a wooden spoon until mixture is creamy and begins to thicken. Working rapidly, drop by rounded tablespoonfuls onto waxed paper; let cool. Yield: about 2 dozen.

A praline vendor is seen in this detail from a painting of the Parade of Volunteer Firemen, New Orleans, 1872.

PEANUT PATTIES

2½ cups sugar
1 cup evaporated milk
⅔ cup light corn syrup
3 cups raw peanuts
1 tablespoon butter
1 teaspoon vanilla extract

Combine sugar, milk, syrup, and peanuts in a small Dutch oven. Slowly bring to a boil, stirring until sugar dissolves. Cover and continue to cook over medium heat 2 to 3 minutes to wash down sugar crystals from sides of pan. Uncover and cook, without stirring, until mixture reaches soft ball stage (234°).

Remove from heat. Add butter and vanilla (do not stir). Let cool to lukewarm (110°). Beat with a wooden spoon until mixture begins to thicken. Drop by tablespoonfuls onto waxed paper; let cool completely. Store in airtight containers in a cool place. Yield: about 3 dozen.

A productive coconut grove, c.1900.

The praline originated in France, where it was merely candy-coated almonds. New Orleans changed all that; what we now expect is a kind of fudge with a delicate grain. It differs from fudge mainly in that it is beaten while hot, whereas fudge is usually cooled to about 110° before beating. And even though pralines may be made with a variety of nuts, many Southerners have come to expect the crunch of their native pecan when they bite into these delicacies. Pralines are more attractive dropped into buttered forms, such as cupcake tins or foil rounds. They are prime gift offerings.

About
    with
Fondar
    1¼ po
    dippi

Drai
towels

Melt
ble boil
stirrin
from h
hot wa

Hold
stem,
allowi
into bo
and le
until s

Plac
bowl t
hot w
melts.

Hol
cherry
choc
drain

Pla
paper
or un
conta
about

PEANUT BUTTER CUPS

1 cup butter or margarine, softened
4½ cups sifted powdered sugar
1 cup creamy peanut butter
2 tablespoons water
4 (8-ounce) packages semisweet chocolate squares

Cream butter in a large mixing bowl; gradually add sugar, beating well. Stir in peanut butter and water. Shape mixture into ½-inch balls. Place on waxed paper-lined baking sheets; set aside.

Place chocolate in top of a double boiler; cook over simmering water, until chocolate melts, stirring well.

Fill paper candy liners one-third full with melted chocolate. Press a peanut butter ball in the center of each liner. Cover top of peanut butter with remaining melted chocolate. Let cool. Store in airtight containers in refrigerator. Yield: about 13 dozen.

DOUBLE PEANUT CLUSTERS

1 (6-ounce) package semisweet chocolate morsels
½ cup creamy peanut butter
1½ cups shelled, roasted peanuts

Combine chocolate and peanut butter in top of a double boiler; cook over simmering water, stirring constantly, until mixture is smooth and creamy. Remove from heat; stir in peanuts. Drop mixture by heaping teaspoonfuls onto waxed paper. Cool completely, and store in an airtight container in refrigerator. Yield: about 2½ dozen.

TEXAS MILLIONAIRES

1 (14-ounce) package caramels
2 teaspoons butter or margarine
2 teaspoons water
3 cups pecan halves
1 (8-ounce) milk chocolate bar

Combine caramels, butter, and water in top of a double boiler; cook over boiling water, stirring constantly, until mixture melts. Remove from heat, leaving mixture over hot water; stir in pecan halves. Spoon 2 caramel-coated pecan halves at a time onto ungreased baking sheets; cool at least 1 hour or until set.

Place chocolate in top of a double boiler over hot water (do not place over heating element). Stir until chocolate melts. Dip each pair of caramel-coated pecan halves in melted chocolate; allow excess to drain.

Place candy on ungreased baking sheets; chill until firm. Arrange candies between layers of waxed paper in airtight containers, and store in a cool place. Yield: about 6 dozen.

HUNKY DORIES

4 cups freshly popped popcorn
1 cup chopped pecans
1 (8-ounce) milk chocolate bar

Combine popcorn and pecans in a large mixing bowl, mixing well; set aside.

Melt chocolate bar in top of a double boiler over simmering water, stirring until chocolate melts.

Pour melted chocolate over reserved popcorn mixture; stir until all popcorn is coated. Drop mixture by tablespoonfuls onto waxed paper-lined cookie sheets; chill until set. Store in airtight containers in a cool place. Yield: 1½ dozen.

Note: Shelled roasted peanuts may be substituted for chopped pecans.

How to enjoy a box of candy, 1890.

1890s trade cards demonstrate an undeniable bond between candy and children

ACKNOWLEDGMENTS

Apricot Balls adapted from *Keneseth Israel Sisterhood Cookbook*, ©1971. By permission of Keneseth Israel Sisterhood, Louisville, Kentucky.

Apricot Mustard adapted from recipes by the Memphis Women's Exchange, Memphis, Tennessee.

Basil Jelly, Papaya Chutney, Summer Vegetable Relish adapted from *La Bonne Cuisine: Cooking New Orleans Style*, compiled by The Women of All Saints' Episcopal Church, ©1981. By permission of La Bonne Cuisine, River Ridge, Louisiana.

Beet-Horseradish Relish, Solger's Truffles, Spiced Plum Butter adapted from *Out of Kentucky Kitchens* by Marion Flexner, ©1949. By permission of Franklin Watts, Inc., New York.

Buttermilk Pralines, Citrus-Candied Pecans adapted from *Caterin' to Charleston* by Gloria Mann Maynard, Meredith Maynard Chase, and Holly Maynard Jenkins, ©1981. By permission of Merritt Publishing Co., Charleston, South Carolina.

Butterscotch Sauce, Caramel Sauce, Sherry Sauce adapted from *Georgia Heritage: Treasured Recipes* by The National Society of The Colonial Dames of America in the State of Georgia, ©1979. By permission of The National Society of The Colonial Dames of America, Savannah, Georgia.

Candied Pineapple and Cherries adapted from *The Mississippi Cookbook*, compiled and edited by the Home Economics Division of the Mississippi Cooperative Extension Service, ©1972. By permission of University Press of Mississippi, Jackson.

Caramelts, Frosted Pecans adapted from *James K. Polk Cookbook*, ©1978. By permission of The James K. Polk Memorial Auxiliary, Columbia, Tennessee.

Chile Salsa adapted from *Seasoned with Sun* by the Junior League of El Paso, ©1974. By permission of the Junior League of El Paso, Inc., Texas.

Citrus Conserve, Kumquat Jelly, Orange-Lemon Marmalade adapted from *Using Florida Fruit* by the Florida Cooperative Extension Service, University of Florida, Gainesville.

Coffee Divinity, Cucumber Relish, Sour Cream Fudge, Spiced Mangos, Tiny Pickled Onions adapted from *State Fair of Texas Prize-Winning Recipes*, compiled and edited by Elizabeth Peabody. By permission of the State Fair of Texas, Dallas.

Coffee Pecans, Georgia Nuggets, Orange-Candied Pecans, President Street Penuche adapted from *Savannah Sampler Cookbook* by Margaret Wayt DeBolt, ©1978. By permission of The Donning Company/Publishers, Inc., Norfolk, Virginia.

Cracker Jacks courtesy of Ms. Marian Williams, Bartlesville, Oklahoma.

Cranberry-Orange Relish adapted from *Woodlawn Plantation Cookbook* by Historic Woodlawn Preservation, ©1979. Courtesy of Woodlawn Plantation Council, National Trust for Historic Preservation, Mt. Vernon, Virginia.

Dilly Beans adapted from *Commonwealth Cupboard*, ©1983, Virginia Department of Agriculture and Consumer Service, Richmond, Virginia.

Fig Jam, Old-Fashioned Apple Butter, Old-Fashioned Peach Butter, Peach Conserve, Pickled Carrots, Pickled Figs, Pickled Peaches, Pickled Pears, Spiced Peach Jam, Spicy Pineapple Sticks, and general pickling and preserving information adapted from *Ball Blue Book*, Edition 31, Ball Corporation, Muncie, Indiana, 1984.

Fresh Fruit Conserve, Peach Relish, Pear Relish adapted from *The Jackson Cookbook* by the Symphony League of Jackson, ©1971. By permission of the Symphony League of Jackson, Mississippi.

Grape Butter adapted from *So Easy to Preserve* by the Cooperative Extension Service, The University of Georgia, Athens, 1984.

Green Tomato Mincemeat, Violet Vinegar adapted from *Welcome Back to Pleasant Hill* by Elizabeth C. Kremer, ©1977. By permission of Shakertown at Pleasant Hill, Harrodsburg, Kentucky.

Green Tomato Pickles, Mango Chutney, Zucchini Pickles adapted from *Pickling Florida Fruits and Vegetables* by the Florida Cooperative Extension Service, University of Florida, Gainesville, 1975.

Herbes Aromatiques, Sweet Hot Mustard adapted from *Delicioso!: Cooking South Texas Style* by the Junior League of Corpus Christi, ©1982. By permission of the Junior League of Corpus Christi, Inc., Texas.

Honey-Pistachio Nougat adapted from *Charleston Receipts*, collected by The Junior League of Charleston, ©1950. By permission of The Junior League of Charleston, South Carolina.

Hot Fudge Sauce courtesy of Mrs. Carol Turner, Chesapeake, Virginia.

Mustard Spread, Squash Relish, Tomato Relish, adapted from *Revel* by The Junior League of Shreveport, Inc., ©1980. By permission of Books Unlimited, Shreveport, Louisiana.

Orange Sauce adapted from *Frances Virginia Tearoom Cookbook* by Mildred Huff Coleman, ©1982. By permission of Peachtree Publishers Limited, Atlanta, Georgia.

Peanut Brittle Wreath courtesy of Ms. Elise Holifield, Marion, Alabama.

Pear Marmalade Magnolia courtesy of Chef Scott Wilson, Magnolia Inn Restaurant, Grove Hill, Alabama.

Pear Mincemeat, Pickled Watermelon Rind adapted from *Food Preservation in Alabama* by the Alabama Cooperative Extension Service, Auburn, Alabama, 1984.

Pickled Jalapeño Peppers adapted from recipes by the Dallas County Extension Agents, Home Economics Division, Dallas, Texas.

Plum Conserve adapted from *Kerr Home Canning and Freezing Book*, ©1983, Kerr Glass Manufacturing Corporation, Consumer Product Division, Los Angeles, California.

Raspberry Truffles, Strawberry Jam, Sugar & Spice Nuts adapted from recipes by Dixie Crystals Sugar.

Squash Pickles courtesy of Mrs. Ed Brown, Pine Bluff, Arkansas.

Sweet Cucumber Rings courtesy of Mrs. Roy Hare, Grove Hill, Alabama.

Collection of Bonnie Slotnick

INDEX